South West by Rail

Dorset
DT1 2HB
Tel. 01305 262659

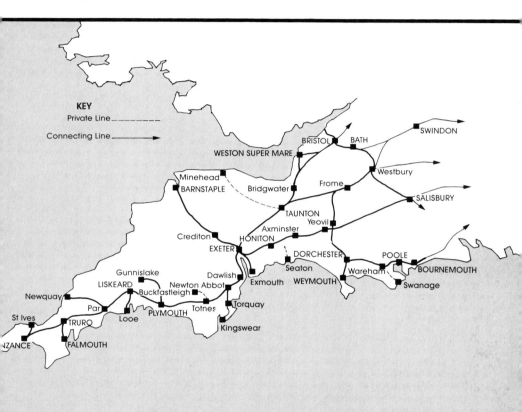

A guide to the routes, scenery and towns

ABOUT THIS BOOK

South West by Rail is one of a series of guidebooks compiled by the Railway Development Society, the independent voluntary body for rail-users.

We invite you to explore this beautiful region by train, with some suggestions for further excursions by bus, bicycle, or on foot from various railheads.

As Editor, I am grateful to all the local members of the Society and its affiliated groups who have contributed so knowledgeably to the book. Thanks are also due to the photographers whose work we have used; to Steven Binks for the line diagrams and Peter Wakefield for the map; and to Geoffrey Burgess, Chris Webb, Eric Barbery, Steve Dymond, John Brodribb, and Ian Carter for help in various ways and to Ron Bond for reading the proofs.

We have written with the general reader in mind, but the inclusion of a few specialised railway terms was unavoidable. The up line or platform is that used by trains travelling towards London; the down line being the opposite. 'DMU' stands for diesel multiple-unit or railcar – the type of train found on most local services. 'InterCity 125' or 'High Speed Train' is the powerful express train operating most long-distance services on the Western Region.

In the diagrams of individual lines, capital letters indicate a staffed station, small print an unstaffed one.

Every effort has been made to include up-to-date information, but we shall be pleased to receive any comments or corrections for incorporation in any future edition.

Trevor Garrod

Front Cover: A High Speed Train leaves Bath Spa (*Photo:* Chris Phillips)
Back cover: Weymouth Harbour (*Photo:* John Brooks)
Inside front cover: Kingswear Marina and Dartmouth (*Photo:* Charles A. Brown)
Inside back cover: Barnstaple (*Photo:* Neil Jinkerson)

CONTENTS

About this book	2
Editor's Introduction	4
Bristol–Taunton–Exeter by Philip Bisatt	5
(London)–Westbury–Taunton by Philip Bisatt	9
(London Waterloo)–Salisbury–Exeter by Jon Honeysett	10
Bournemouth–Weymouth by Trevor Garrod	13
City of Bristol by Geoff Mills	16
Bristol–Severn Beach by Owen Prosser	18
Bristol–Bath–Westbury by Chris Phillips	20
Salisbury–Westbury Jon Honeysett	21
Swanage by Trevor Garrod	22
Castle Cary–Yeovil–Dorchester by John Penny	24
West Somerset Railway by Alan Harwood	26
Exeter–Exmouth by Joan Fuller	30
Exeter–Barnstaple by Ian Dinmore	33
Exeter–Torquay–Plymouth by Fiona West	35
Torbay & Dartmouth Railway by Richard Jones	38
Dart Valley Railway by Richard Jones	40
City of Plymouth by Phoebe Lean	42
Plymouth–Gunnislake by Clive Charlton	44
Plymouth–Penzance by Noel Sloman	48
Liskeard–Looe by Clive Davies	54
Par–Newquay Graham Townsend	56
Truro–Falmouth by Noel Sloman	58
St Erth–St Ives by Clive Davies	59
Further Information	62
What is the Railway Development Society?	63
Index	64

EDITOR'S INTRODUCTION

The four south-western counties of Devon and Cornwall, Somerset and Dorset, have long been one of England's most popular holiday areas – and understandably so, with their long coastlines, attractive scenery, interesting market towns and fishing ports, cathedral cities and picturesque villages.

Two mainline railway companies, the Great Western Railway and the London & South Western Railway, vied with each other to build trunk routes into the South West with branches to its many small towns and resorts.

Despite line closures in the 1950s and 1960s, over 630 miles of passenger railway remain to serve this region. High Speed Trains travelling at up to 125mph link it to London, the Midlands, and the North; while diesel multiple-units and locomotive-hauled trains run on more than a dozen branches and cross-country lines. New trains are starting to appear on these routes, and more are promised.

Since 1970, the area has seen a modest railway revival, with stations opened, or new ones built, at Feniton, Templecombe, Pinhoe, Lympstone Commando, Falmouth, Lelant Saltings, and Melksham – and there is scope for more. Preservation Societies have reopened the lines to Minehead, Kingswear, and Buckfastleigh with vintage steam and diesel trains. Buses with through ticketing run from the nearest railheads to the resorts of Lyme Regis, Seaton, Sidmouth, Ilfracombe, Bideford, Bude, and Padstow. Swanage has both a rail-link bus service and the start of a preserved line. Rail excursions are sometimes run on the freight line to Okehampton.

From a window-seat in the train you can view the stately stone city of Bath in its green valley; the breezy Dorset Downs and the wild edges of Dartmoor; the beautiful harbours of Poole, Plymouth, and Falmouth; while few main-line railways give you such a spectacular run between cliffs and open sea as this one does at Dawlish; and few branches such idyllic rides past woods and water as those to Looe and Gunnislake.

Alight and sample the cider and the cream teas of this lush region; follow in the footsteps of Drake and Raleigh; admire the fine Honiton lace and Axminster carpets; marvel at Chesil Beach and St Michael's Mount; visit the places immortalised in Thomas Hardy's novels and the monuments to the engineering skill of Isambard Kingdom Brunel.

Your interesting voyage of discovery will, we believe, show you the value of the railways of the South West and the case for their retention and further development.

Trevor Garrod

High Speed Train passes Westbury White Horse. (*Photo:* Rod Muncey)

BRISTOL–TAUNTON–EXETER
by Philip Bisatt

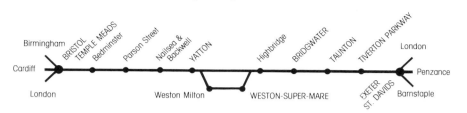

For many travellers, Bristol Temple Meads is the gateway to the South West, with InterCity 125 trains going onward to Torbay, Plymouth, and Penzance, while local services radiate to Weston-super-Mare, Taunton, Salisbury, Weymouth, and Severn Beach.

It is worth pausing for a few moments to study Temple Meads Station. If you are approaching from the city, Brunel's original terminus (which can be visited) is on the left-hand side of the forecourt, while opposite are the 1847 Bristol & Exeter Railway offices, now used by the British Rail Area Manager. The imposing clock tower and main frontage were added later as part of a scheme to link the previously separate Great Western and Bristol & Exeter stations.

For those seeking refreshment, the Merchant Venturer buffet/bar on Platform 3 provides an elegant resting place. Trains for the South West generally use Platforms 7–12, beyond the overall roof. InterCity services are fairly frequent and are supplemented by local services calling at all intermediate stations to Weston-super-Mare and Taunton.

Leaving Temple Meads our train passes through a somewhat run-down area of Bristol, with stations at Bedminster and Parson Street. The Freightliner depot soon comes into view on the right and in the distance beyond may be seen Brunel's Clifton Suspension Bridge, spanning the Avon Gorge.

We then enter open countryside and, after passing through the short Flax Bourton Tunnel, have a downhill run to the next station, Nailsea and Backwell, serving two separate but adjoining settlements. Backwell lies next to the station, while Nailsea is ½-mile away to our right. On weekdays a fair number of local people use the train to travel to work in Bristol.

Soon the isolated church and manor house of Chelvey can be seen on the left, followed by the grounds of Nailsea Court to our right. For the next few miles the line is almost completely straight, crossing what are known as the 'Northern Levels', to distinguish them from those farther south, in Somerset.

Yatton, the next station, is still staffed and has pleasant stone buildings. At one time it was a busy junction, with branches to Clevedon and Wells, but unfortunately both lines were closed in the 1960s, depriving quite large towns of rail services. Nowadays Clevedon with a population of 20,000 relies on Yatton as a railhead, though frustratingly there are no connecting bus services. Fortunately, Avon County Council have funded improved facilities for those wishing to 'park and ride'.

More straight track lies ahead until we pass under the M5 motorway and take the loop line into Weston-super-Mare. Before reaching the main station we pass Weston Milton Halt, used mainly by Bristol commuters. Many fast trains do not, in fact, call at Weston but instead use the 'avoiding line' which actually predates the town loop by over forty years!

Bristol Temple Meads Station. (*Photo:* Philip Bisatt)

It is difficult to realise that Weston-super-Mare with its population of 70,000 is entirely a modern creation. In 1800 it was a small fishing village, but the arrival of the railway led to it becoming a fashionable resort. The seafront is ten minutes' walk from the station and those seeking sand will find no shortage! Birnbeck Pier, in the north of the town, is well worth visiting and pleasant walks are to be had on Worlebury Hill. The Grand Pier offers the more commercial kinds of seaside amusements.

Bus services from Weston will take you to Cheddar, with its famous gorge and caves; to Wells and its cathedral; and to a host of other places. Most buses are operated by Badgerline.

Leaving Weston-super-Mare, we pass through a large housing estate before rejoining the main line. After a short but deep cutting we enter the Somerset Levels which stretch most of the way to Taunton. The 'Levels' are a low-lying coastal belt of clay, parts of which have been reclaimed from the sea. Between Weston and Highbridge a number of minor roads cross the railway on embanked bridges, the earth for which was dug from adjoining land. This has led to the formation of small ponds in these 'borrow pits', which are now valuable wildlife habitats.

The unmistakeable feature of Brent Knoll is seen on our left as we approach Highbridge, whose station acts as a railhead for the resort of Burnham-on-Sea and serves about 18,000 people. Unfortunately the station buildings have all been demolished, leaving only rudimentary shelter, and there are no connecting buses to Burnham-on-Sea, although an hourly service does operate along Church Street, 200 yards from the station approach. Currently Highbridge enjoys rather a limited train service and one can only hope for improvements, especially as rapid population growth is taking place in the area.

We continue across the Levels, roughly parallel to the M5 motorway, crossing after a couple of miles the Huntspill River, an artificial drainage channel cut in 1940 to drain the central Somerset Moors, and the similar Kings Sedgemoor Drain at Dunball.

As we approach Bridgwater, industry and warehousing come into view on the right, unfortunately not rail-connected. On our left are the British Cellophane works, opened in 1935 partly to offset unemployment in local brick and tile industries. This factory does have rail sidings, used for moving chemicals by Speedlink freight trains.

Bridgwater Station was repainted in 1985 with help from Sedgemoor District Council. The train service is not, perhaps, as good as one would hope for a town of 31,000 people, but local trains are quite well patronised. A few InterCity services also call.

The town centre is ten minutes' walk from the station, across the River Parrett. Until the 1960's Bridgwater was a commercial port, and the dock area has been attractively converted to provide new housing and a marina. If you are feeling thirsty, try the Admiral's Landing bar in the former dock warehouse! Bridgwater was the birthplace of the Cromwellian seaman Robert Blake, whose statue is in the town centre. Bear right here into High Street for the Tourist Information Centre.

Our train heads south, crossing the River Parrett, speeding under the M5 and passing flooded clay workings that are a legacy of the now-defunct brick industry. To our right the Bridgwater & Taunton Canal runs roughly parallel to the railway for much of its length. The train now crosses the edge of North Moor which, with its distinctive pollarded willows, rhynes (ditches), and rough pasture is noticeably different in character to the Levels. Much of North Moor is of international importance for wildlife, and has been designated a Site of Special Scientific Interest (SSSI) by the Nature Conservancy Council.

A short cutting brings us to the main London—West of England route at Cogload Junction, 5 miles east of Taunton, which we were soon approaching after passing once again under the M5. Once a very busy junction with branches to Chard Yeovil, Barnstaple, and Minehead, Taunton Station is now a railhead for a large part of Somerset as a result of over-zealous wielding of the axe by Dr Beeching and successive Ministers of Transport. Fortunately, InterCity services to London, the Midlands, and the South West remain frequent.

Taunton is Somerset's county town, with a population of 50,000. The station is some distance from the town centre, but on weekdays a frequent shuttle minibus service links the two. Alight at the Parade for the central shopping area and the Castle with its Museum. Taunton has several fine churches, notably St Mary's (sixteenth century) and is also well supplied with places to eat and drink—at varying prices!

From Taunton it is another 31 miles to Exeter, and InterCity 125 trains cover this distance in less than half an hour. There are also locomotive-hauled trains on this section, particularly on summer Saturdays, linking the South West with the Midlands and North. There are at present, however, no stopping services, all local stations having been closed in 1964.

Leaving Taunton, we pass one of its well-known public schools on the right and Fairwater sidings on the left. After a busy Silk Mill level crossing, a line diverges to the right to serve the Taunton Cider Company, an important Railfreight customer which dispatches its products by rail to the North of England, Scotland and Northern Ireland.

Our train now heads through pleasantly undulating countryside. The derelict remains of the Grand Western Canal may be glimpsed from time to time, particularly an embanked section to the left of the railway. Like many others this canal, which ran from Taunton to Tiverton, was bought up by the railway company and fell into disuse in the 1960s. However, the section between Tiverton and the Devon/Somerset border remains open for occasional pleasure-boats.

We can see in the distance on our left the Blackdown Hills and, of particular interest, the monument to the Duke of Wellington, erected in 1817 after the Battle of Waterloo. The town of Wellington (whence came the Duke's title) is soon reached, signified by the Relyon bed factory to the left of the Railway. There has been local pressure to reopen Wellington Station and restore rail services to a town of 11,000 people.

After Wellington, our train begins a 3-mile climb to Whiteball summit, passing under the A38 road bridge *en route*. The summit lies just beyond Whiteball Tunnel, which straddles the Somerset/Devon county boundary. Now it is downhill all the way to Exeter. A couple of miles beyond Whiteball, to the right of the railway, can be seen the still-operable section of the Grand Western Canal. In the distance beyond it is Westleigh Quarry which was once served by a branch from the main line.

The M5 comes in from the left and we pass under the North Devon link road bridge before reaching Tiverton Parkway Station. Opened in May 1986, this station is a good example of a joint venture between British Rail and the local authorities – in this case Devon County and Mid-Devon District Councils. Patronage so far has been good: modern passenger facilities and generous car parking encourage people to 'park and ride'. The sizeable town of Tiverton lies 6 miles to the west, but for those without a car, a connecting bus service is available, thanks to the support of Devon County Council. Another bus service operates to Cullompton, 5 miles to the south.

Our train now runs parallel to the M5, passing the former Tiverton Junction Station, which was replaced by Parkway. A couple of miles further on, the expanding town of Cullompton can be seen on our right. There have been suggestions that the station here might reopen, but this now seems less likely following the construction of Tiverton Parkway.

As its name suggests, Cullompton lies in the valley of the River Culm, which we pick up here and follow for about 8 miles. The M5 remains on our left, taking a parallel course to the railway but with much greater environmental impact. The railway twists and turns as it follows the Culm, requiring a modest restriction in speed to 75mph along this section. How many motorists can you see overhauling us?

A little farther on, rail and road part company. We continue to follow the Culm for another 5 miles, passing on our right the maroon-clad paper mill at Hele, formerly rail-connected. A wooded hill can be seen on our left – part of the grounds of Killerton House and now owned by the National Trust.

Soon the valley opens out and we enter a rich farming area, characterised by large open fields and few trees. The large village of Stoke Canon can then be seen to the left of the railway. It had a station until 1964 and the Exe Valley line linking Exeter to Tiverton used to diverge a this point. Beyond the village the Culm joins the River Exe, which we follow closely for the remainder of the route to Exeter. One the left are Stoke Woods, a large area of woodland which, unfortunately, is being progressively felled and replaced by conifer plantations.

At Cowley Bridge Junction, the Barnstaple line trails in from the right. The clatter of pointwork (for those who still notice these things in the quieter environment of a High Speed Train) indicates we are approaching Exeter. On our right can be seen Exeter Riverside marshalling yard, which handles much of Railfreight's traffic to and from the South West. We enter Exeter St David's Station over a very wide level crossing, which for reasons of public safety has to be permanently manned.

Exeter St David's has always been the most important station west of Bristol, with lines radiating to Salisbury, Barnstaple, Exmouth, and the South West. A wide variety of freight is also handled here. For those wishing to visit the city centre, trains to the more convenient Central Station leave from Platforms 1 and 3; while refreshments can be obtained on Platforms 1 and 5.

(LONDON)–WESTBURY–TAUNTON
by Philip Bisatt

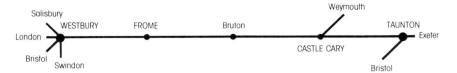

Westbury has been an important railway junction for more than a century, particularly since the completion of the direct London–Taunton route in 1906. InterCity trains on this main line to the West of England call at Westbury every two hours; and passenger services radiate to Bath and Bristol; Salisbury, Southampton, and Portsmouth; Yeovil and Weymouth; and there is a limited service to Swindon via the reopened station at Melksham. The absence of InterCity services at Trowbridge, Warminster and Frome means that Westbury also acts as railhead for a large part of East Somerset and West Wiltshire.

At present there are no local trains between Westbury and Taunton, so we must take an InterCity 125 for the 47-mile journey. Leaving Westbury, we pass the extensive sidings, which may be full of local freight traffic–limestone, cement, bitumen, and roadstone–before the Westbury avoiding line (for non-stopping trains) rejoins us at Fairwood Junction. After a brief run through undulating pastoral countryside, we pass the outskirts of Frome. The station here is on a loop line to our right, and is currently only served by Weymouth line trains plus a solitary evening one from London. However, as Frome is the largest settlement between Reading and Taunton, with a population of 23,000, there has been considerable pressure to upgrade its station to InterCity status.

For the moment, though, we speed past on the avoiding line and enter an area of attractive, thinly populated countryside. After about 5 miles we pass the site of Witham Station, where the busy freight line to Merehead Quarry diverges to the right. At one time this branch continued through to Yatton, serving Shepton Mallet and Wells.

Soon after Witham, our train begins the downhill run from Brewham summit towards Bruton. On one of the hills to our left may be seen Alfred's Tower, an eighteenth century folly erected on the Stourhead estate and now owned by the National Trust. We pass through pleasant wooded countryside on the approach to Bruton, a small stone-built town to the right of the railway, probably best known for its public school–Kings. Its station is unstaffed and served only by Weymouth line trains.

A couple of miles beyond Bruton, the valley opens out and we soon reach Castle Cary Station, a stop for some InterCity trains as well as all those to Weymouth. This station is still manned and is indeed very well cared for. Castle Cary itself sits on top of the hill to the south of the railway. It is a small town of less than 3,000 people, but its station acts as railhead for a very large area–mainly because of the exceptionally severe rail cuts made in Somerset in the 1960s.

The single-track line to Weymouth diverges immediately beyond Castle Cary. We take the main line to Taunton, opened by the Great Western Railway in 1906. For a few miles we pass through rather open, unremarkable countryside, across which, at one point, Glastonbury Tor may be observed on the horizon to our right.

Then the scenery changes as we enter the Cary Valley, a couple of miles east of Somerton. Our train follows the right-hand side of the valley on a high embankment, before swinging left to cross the River Cary on a tall viaduct. Next we enter a rocky cutting which actually bisects the town of Somerton, a place of some antiquity which lost its station in 1962. There has been local pressure to reopen it, however, and the large number of new houses bears witness to rapid population growth. Notice the simulated stone used in their construction, in an attempt to match the local Blue Lias traditionally used for building in this area.

The next feature of note is Somerton Tunnel, interestingly enough the only one in the 143 miles between London and Taunton. Beyond the tunnel the train runs across the grain of the countryside – over embankments and through rock cuttings before passing Langport, a rapidly expanding little town which once boasted two stations, both of which, alas, were closed in 1964. Here is another case for possible reopening.

After Langport the scenery changes dramatically as we cross the River Parrett on a viaduct and enter the Somerset Levels and Moors. This part of the moors used to suffer severe flooding; indeed in 1894 water reached the upper windows of houses in Langport. Thanks to modern drainage schemes, conditions are much improved, although even today it is not uncommon to see the moors transformed into shallow lakes in winter. One of the sluices used to regulate the local drainage system may be observed on the right a couple of miles beyond Langport.

On our left, a range of wooded hills can be seen bordering the moors. At one point on their summit is the Burton Pynsent monument, erected in the eighteenth century at the behest of William Pitt the Younger. It is said that a cow managed to climb the stairs inside, as a result of which the tower was sealed. There are currently plans to restore and reopen it.

We pass through a short cutting and continue across the moors towards the level crossing at Athelney, reputed to be the place where Alfred burnt the cakes. In the distance to our right can be seen Burrow Mump, a conical hill crowned by a ruined church, and which may have been used by Alfred as a fort. At Athelney we cross the River Tone and swing left past the village of East Lyng, which like many others sits on flood-free ground above the moors. Soon we reach Cogload Junction, where we join the line from Bristol for the last 5 miles to Taunton. The remainder of this route to the South West is described on page 5.

(LONDON WATERLOO) – SALISBURY – EXETER
by Jon Honeysett

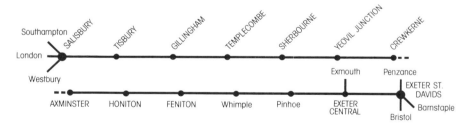

This is one of the three main routes to the West Country – the former London & South Western Railway line from London Waterloo via Basingstoke, Andover, Salisbury, Yeovil Junction, and Honiton to Exeter Central and Exeter St Davids.

The rival ex-Great Western Railway routes now have High Speed Trains operating services through Penzance from London, the Midlands, and the North, including the famous 'Cornish Riviera' and 'Torbay Express' from Paddington, maintaining the reputation for speed and comfort set by their steam predecessors. The L & SWR route has, by contrast, felt the effects of economic uncertainty, particularly through the

'Beeching years', but is now experiencing something of a comeback.

The route west of Salisbury traverses some of the most beautiful of the Wessex countryside, which until 1964 resounded to the pounding exhausts of the big Bulleid Pacific steam locomotives, as they hurried their heavy 'portioned expresses' from Waterloo to the towns and resorts of East Devon, North Cornwall, and North Devon, and even younger travellers will have heard of the most famous of these trains – 'The Atlantic Coast Express'. Now the lines to places like Padstow, Bude and Ilfracombe have closed and the trains from Waterloo terminate at Exeter – though the Railway Development Society believes there is a case for extending possibly two a day on to Barnstaple, thus giving the North Devon line a through service from London and the South East.

The south-western route to the West Country is able to offer Waterloo to Exeter expresses every two hours nowadays, composed of comfortable Mark II coaches hauled by powerful Class 50 diesel-electric locomotives, each named after warships of the Royal Navy that once proudly sailed from Devonport. At thirty-seven minutes past every even hour, a London Waterloo – Exeter St Davids express pulls away from Salisbury's Platform 4, to begin its 90-mile run to the West. Let us join one, and sample the route for ourselves.

As the famous cathedral spire recedes over the rooftops, our train runs through a chalk cutting until, some 2 miles west, the double-track main line to Westbury and Bristol diverges at Wilton. Over the tree-tops can be seen the roof of Wilton House, well worth a visit. Our line changes to single track as it follows the meandering course of the Hampshire Avon's tributary, the clear-watered River Nadder. Beyond the thatched cottages of Barford St Martin, one can discern the northern rim of Cranborne Chase, into whose chalk escarpments are carved the regimental badges of the old British Army that was decimated on the similar terrain of Northern France and Belgium in that 'War to end all wars' from 1914 to 1918.

For ramblers and cyclists, this countryside is excellent – long unspoiled views from many small lanes, that rejoice to the song of the lark and the bleating of sheep, while those students of pre-Roman history will find themselves among tumuli and groups of earthworks. The first two stations at which we stop, Tisbury and Gillingham, are ideal starting-points for travellers to Wessex, and are close to picturesque Shaftesbury.

At Tisbury is a passing loop, reinstated in 1986 to enable two trains to pass one another on what was previously a very long single-track section. The line had been singled in the 1960s as an economy measure; and the building of this loop, to improve punctuality, is the first of a number of signs we shall see of the line's renaissance.

From Gillingham our train begins the long ascent to Buckhorn Weston Tunnel, from which it emerges to glorious views of Blackmore Vale. At Templecombe we pause, at a station which was once the junction with the old Somerset & Dorset Joint Railway, which ran from Bournemouth to Bath. Only the trackbed of the Somerset & Dorset now remains, passing under our line, but Templecombe Station itself represents another forward step. It was closed in the 1960s, but reopened for excursion trains in the early 1980s and then reopened permanently in 1984, thanks to the efforts of a local action group.

The section from Templecombe to Sherborne and Yeovil Junction reverts to double track, and soon the ruins of Sherborne Abbey can be viewed just south of the town itself. Those interested in architecture will have noticed the subtle change in building material – where North Hampshire and Wiltshire has a mix of red brick and flint-lining, Dorset and Somerset has the influence of Mendip and Portland stone – the chalk lands have given way to the Jurassic limestone strata of the region.

As we approach the wide cutting in which lies Yeovil Junction, the now-singled line from Weymouth to Yeovil Pen Mill, Castle Cary, and Westbury can be seen passing at right angles underneath. This former GWR line still has a connecting spur to our route,

Waterloo–Exeter train west of Yeovil Junction. (*Photo:* Tom Heavyside)

and is occasionally used by services diverted because of engineering work, and by engineers' trains.

Yeovil Junction Station has a bus service to the town and there are taxis. Yeovil itself is described on page 25. At nearby Yeovilton is the Fleet Air Arm Museum, housing a superb collection of vintage and modern aircraft; and of interest to rail 'buffs' is the working turntable in the former down siding at Yeovil Junction.

On single track again, our Class 50 heads west to Crewkerne, jumping-off point for devotees of Thomas Hardy. South of this little station, a lonely road winds up into the western edge of Wessex, to Beaminster and the Channel coast at Bridport–the high farmlands, copses and gorse-strewn common land evoke memories of 'Tess of the D'Urbervilles' and the downtrodden peasantry who rose up in rebellion with Monmouth, who were to be hounded into transportation hulks or ruthlessly press-ganged–Wessex as a regional entity finds echoes of sympathy in this area.

Now, dear traveller, the countryside changes again, as we enter the Triassic sandstone of East Devon. The contours of the hills become more pronounced as our train thunders past the Milk Marketing Board depot at what was once Chard Junction, with its rows of glass-lined milk-tanker wagons, to Axminster.

From this town, world famous for its carpets, buses make their way to Lyme Regis (where in steam days an elegant but elderly Adams radial tank engine would haul its two-coach train along the branch to that resort's hill-top terminus), and down the Axe Valley to Seaton which, views apart, has much to offer the visitor. On the track of the old branch line, closed like that to Lyme Regis in the 1960s, there now runs for 3 miles a unique narrow-gauge electric tramway, linking Seaton with the small town of Colyford, 3 miles inland. This pleasant run along the valleys of the rivers Axe and Coly, with their varied bird life, is available daily from Easter to the end of October, with a more limited service in winter. (For details write to the General Manager, Seaton Tramway, Harbour

Road, Seaton, Devon EX12 2NQ, or telephone 0297–21702.) On the western edge of Seaton is the Beer Heights Railway, set in the hillside premises of the Peco Model Railway factory.

Returning to the main line, the stiffest of climbs now confronts our Class 50, as it winds our train past the site of Seaton Junction to ascend Honiton bank. On these heights it is possible to see buzzards floating in the up draughts. Cresting the summit into Honiton itself, we come to a halt in the lace-making town where passengers for Sidmouth need to alight for a bus connection.

From here to Exeter is mostly 'down gradient', through Feniton, a station reopened in 1971 on the site of the former Sidmouth Junction, Whimple and its cider orchards, and Pinhoe, the third reopened (in 1984) station on this route, serving the eastern suburbs of Exeter.

At Exmouth Junction, the branch to Exmouth curves in from our left, while on our right a few wagon sidings mark the site of the former motive power depot, where once main-line steam-engines were coaled and watered ready for their arduous duties.

After a brief descent into Exeter Central, our train pauses for Exmouth passengers to join the diesel multiple-unit service to that pleasant seaside town, described on page 33. Older travellers are reminiscing of the days when the 'portioned expresses' were divided here – the bustle of activity as massive Z Class tank engines banked the eastbound trains up the steep slope from Exeter St Davids and I, as a young Senior Aircraftsman, bound for my base at RAF Chivenor, west of Barnstaple, had to ensure I was in my correct Ilfracombe portion!

Nowadays Exeter Central is a quieter place, but the most convenient station for the historic city centre. Our train then drops the steep curving bank, across the River Exe, to terminate in the busy Exeter St Davids Station. Our journey is at an end, after two hours of good travelling, yet perhaps for you it is the beginning of a realisation of the joys of 'South West by Rail'.

BOURNEMOUTH–WEYMOUTH
by Trevor Garrod

Bournemouth, with its sandy beaches and wooded cliffs on which stand well-appointed hotels and apartment blocks, is one of the leading resorts of the South Coast. The town and its suburbs stretch for 10 miles along the coast and its pleasant setting has also made it a favourite place in which to hold major conferences and in which to retire.

But Bournemouth is also a gateway for exploring the county of Dorset. The main line from London Waterloo, electrified in 1967, enjoys three trains every hour throughout the day. The fastest call at only two stations and cover the 108 miles in ninety-eight minutes. Through trains also run from such places as Birmingham, Liverpool, Newcastle and Glasgow to Bournemouth and neighbouring Poole.

The line west of Bournemouth, into the heart of Dorset, is now being electrified – but for the past two decades it has seen a type of service unique on British Rail. Four or eight coaches of the electric multiple-unit train from London have been hauled westwards over the non-electrified line as far as Weymouth by a diesel locomotive – which then pushes

Wareham – a pleasant town served by the Bournemouth–Weymouth line. (*Photo:* John Brooks)

them back to Bournemouth! Thus quite small places like Wareham and Dorchester enjoy a remarkably good through service to the capital.

The train leaves Bournemouth's imposing central station (currently subject to possible redevelopment plans by the British Rail Property Board) and runs through hilly wooded suburbs that could be 'stockbroker Surrey' – for the sea is largely out of sight behind the trees – until the blue waters of Poole's great natural harbour come into view. We pass an attractive boating lake on the right, while across the harbour to the left is Brownsea Island, site of the original Boy Scouts camp in 1907 and now a nature reserve, which can be visited on a seasonal ferry from Poole.

A sharp curve brings us into Poole's reconstructed station, dominated on the landward side by a complex of concrete roadways, multi-storey car parks, modern office blocks, and a shopping centre. Soon we are curving westwards again, crossing Holes Bay on a causeway and calling at Hamworthy Station, from which a freight line runs off to the left towards the harbour and power-station.

More attractive views of the harbour and its yachts follow as we run across flat heathland and past pine woods before drawing into the station at Wareham. This small town of 4,000 people is situated just to the south of the line, on rising ground between the rivers Piddle and Frome. It has two interesting medieval churches, boating on the river, and pleasant walks along the course of the old town walls.

Our train continues across the River Piddle and its meadows, through a cutting and past the junction with the former Swanage line, reaching the shallow valley of the River Frome, which it follows for the next 15 miles to Dorchester. A few miles to the south is the smooth ridge of the Purbeck Downs, while the country to the north is more wooded.

The modern station at Wool serves an expanded village, the Army camp at Bovington (with its Tank Museum) just to the north, and the Atomic Energy Establishment at Winfrith – whose neat rectangular blocks set amid lawns and trees come into view on the left and have their own rail connection. Then comes the expanse of Winfrith Heath – part of the 'Egdon Heath' of Thomas Hardy's novels. Some of the heath is now afforested, as round the halt at Moreton, and Puddletown Forest, an attractive area that now comes into view to the north of the river. Thomas Hardy's birthplace is a thatched cottage in the heart of this forest. It is not visible from the train, but there is a good view of the white Stinsford Hall, now the Dorset College of Agriculture.

The line from Moreton to Dorchester has been singled, but as we reach the town's outskirts it again becomes double, and our train soon draws into the curving platforms of South Station, officially opened on 25 November 1986. The original Dorchester South was a terminus, into which trains had to shunt inconveniently. Buildings of this old station have now been incorporated into the adjacent Eldridge Pope brewery, who paid half the cost of the new station.

Dorchester, with a population of 14,000, is not the largest town in Dorset, but it is the county town and an ideal centre for the rail-based tourist. This compact market town has a handsome high street with a good range of inns, shops, and eating-places. There are four museums, including the large Dorset County Museum with geological, archaeological, and natural history departments plus a section on Thomas Hardy and his era. Also worth a visit is the remarkable Dinosaur Museum, where the history of these prehistoric monsters, based partly on local fossil finds, is told by video and computers as well as by more conventional exhibits.

Ancient history is also represented by fragments of a Roman wall and town house and the pre-Roman Maumbury Rings amphitheatre near South Station. For further exploration, call in at the well-stocked Tourist Information Office in Acland Road, whose leaflets include *Dorchester Walks* and *The West Dorset Cycleway*.

The line leaves Dorchester South Station in a cutting and is soon joined by the former Great Western route from Castle Cary. As the train emerges on an embankment, look

Thomas Hardy's cottage near Dorchester. (*Photo:* Neil Jinkerson)

across to the west, where the great grassy earthworks of Maiden Castle, an Iron Age hill-fortress, dominate the skyline and form one of a number of destinations for pleasant walks from Dorchester town.

The train heads south across undulating downland, climbing to Bincombe Tunnel, from which it emerges to begin its long descent to the coast, passing the remains of a platform by the main road. This was Upwey Wishing Well Halt, built to serve the pool that marks the source of the River Wey, twenty minutes' walk to the west, and a popular excursion-point at the turn of the century. Present-day visitors to this beauty-spot must alight at Upwey Station, about a mile farther south, and walk back through the village.

A continuous built-up area stretches alongside the line now, but with views of Radipole Lake to the west. Soon we draw into Weymouth's three-platform station, rebuilt in 1985-86 with a convenient bus interchange. From here it is a mere 100 yards to the broad sandy beach, lined with gracious Georgian buildings and presided over by a large statue of King George III. It was this monarch who did much for Weymouth's reputation as a resort, spending several summers here about the turn of the nineteenth century.

But Weymouth is more than a seaside resort. It is also an ancient port, and ships still ply from here to France and the Channel Islands. A separate railway line branches off just before the main station and runs along the quayside to an island platform right next to the boat.

A third line used to run across the river and down to Portland Island, which is connected to the mainland by a causeway and the remarkable bar of shingle known as 'Chesil Beach'. It is still possible to walk or cycle along part of the trackbed of this line — or you can take a town bus to various points on Portland Island, famous as a naval base and, like Purbeck, back along the coast, the source of stone for buildings in many parts of England.

CITY OF BRISTOL
by Geoff Mills

Bristol's main railway station, Temple Meads, provides a magnificent point of entry to the city. The present station, built in the 1870s in the Gothic style, is a listed building and adjoins Brunel's original station of 1841 which is constructed in Bath stone in a castellated Tudor style. The latter has a superb hammerbeam roof supported on Tudor-style wrought-iron columns and now plays host to exhibitions and sports events instead of trains.

Although suffering heavy bombing during the Second World War, Bristol still retains many fine buildings as well as an attractive harbour and the spectacular Avon Gorge. As Temple Meads is situated on the edge of the central business area and some ¾ mile from the principal shopping centre, Broadmead, the best means by which to reach the major attractions is by bus. With the deregulation of the bus industry services are liable to frequent change, but at the time of writing (December 1986) Services 8 and 9 (City Line) and 510 (Badgerline) depart from just outside the Station entrance every few minutes and serve both the Broadmead and Queens Road shopping centres. Services 8 and 9 also serve The Centre (for the harbour), College Green (for the Cathedral), and Clifton (for the village, Downs, Zoo and Suspension Bridge).

Broadmead was constructed just after the war on an area devastated by bombing. Two of its main streets have been attractively pedestrianised and here and there a few old buildings survive. These include The Arcade 1824-25, a corridor of small shops situated opposite John Lewis's in The Horsefair, which emerges into Broadmead, (the street) adjacent to John Wesley's New Room of 1739, the world's first Methodist church. Nearby in Merchant Street is an attractive court of the Merchant Taylor Almshouses restored in green and white and now a branch of Lloyds Bank. Almost opposite the almshouses is the entrance to Quakers Friars with its collection of medieval and eighteenth-century buildings including the former Quaker meeting-house of 1747-49, where William Penn was married in 1695.

Merchant Street runs into Newgate, on the opposite side of which is the castle mound. The castle was destroyed after the Civil War but its site is now an open grassed area with a view down to the upper reaches of the Floating Harbour and the Courage brewery beyond. Also within this area is the ruin of the bombed St Peter's Church.

Newgate leads uphill into Wine Street which in turn continues into Corn Street and the financial sector of the city. The most distinguished building here is the Corn Exchange built in Palladian style between 1740 and 1743. Between the Exchange and Baldwin Street is an interesting area of markets, warehouses, pubs and restaurants.

Corn Street and Baldwin Street both emerge on The Centre, so called because it used to be the centre of the city's tramway network. It is now served by most of the city's bus services.

At the southern end of The Centre access can be gained to St Augustine's Reach, a section of the Floating Harbour. The former sheds have been restored to create The Watershed, a media and communications centre, and the Bristol Exhibition Centre. On the opposite side of St Augustine's Reach it is possible to walk along Narrow Quay to the Arnolfini Arts Centre and then over the Prince's Street swing bridge to the National Lifeboat Museum and the adjacent Bristol Industrial Museum. The Arnolfini is housed in a splendid former tea warehouse built in 1832. The museums are in more recent sheds standing on the site of Pattersons shipyard where Brunel's famous paddle-steamer The Great Western was built in 1836-38. Beyond the Industrial Museum is the Maritime Heritage Centre together with Brunel's historic ship *The Great Britain*. This ship, the

Bristol steam train beside the Floating Harbour. (*Photo:* Owen Prosser)

largest vessel ever built when launched from this dock in 1843, was also the first ocean-going screw-driven iron ship in the world. For those who prefer not to walk, a bus (Service 511 – Badgerline) operates between The Centre and Hanover Place which is nearby *The Great Britain*.

Close by The Centre, is College Green, which is flanked by the Anglican Cathedral and the Council House. The cathedral dates mainly from the thirteenth and fourteenth centuries although some Norman work has survived and the west front towers are Victorian, completed in 1888. The Council House, built in the late 1930s is in the neo-Georgian style fashionable at that time but its curved frontage and gilt unicorns at either end endow it with some distinction.

From College Green one can either walk or take a bus up Park Street to the Queens Road shopping centre which has many quality and specialised shops. The University, with its impressive 215 foot-high tower, museum, and art gallery are all situated here. A short walk down Berkeley Avenue leads to Brandon Hill open space and the Cabot Tower. The tower, built in 1897 to commemorate the 400th anniversary of the discovery of Newfoundland by John Cabot, offers a superb view over Bristol.

Service 8 continues from Queens Road to Clifton (Service 9 on the return) which contains many Georgian buildings including the longest crescent in England, the modern Roman Catholic Cathedral, the zoo, and Brunel's renowned suspension bridge. The bridge, opened in 1861, spans the Avon Gorge through which the tidal river flows 245 feet below. Close by the bridge are the Clifton and Durdham Downs, an extensive area of open space.

Returning to The Centre, a short distance along Redcliffe Way leads to a roundabout at which the left turn goes into King Street. This is one of the most attractive in Bristol and contains many old buildings, some half timbered, the finest of which is the Llandoger Trow, now a restaurant, but originally a row of houses. A trow is a flat-bottomed Welsh sailing barge and the waterfront at the end of the street is known as 'Welsh Back'. Other buildings of interest include the former public library of 1740, the Coopers' Hall of 1744 which is now the foyer to the Theatre Royal, and the St Nicholas Almshouse of 1652. All pubs in King Street sell real ale.

Turning right into Welsh Back leads to Redcliffe Way from where it is possible to either return to the Centre via Queens Square, or to cross the bridge and return to Temple Meads passing the Church of St Mary Redcliffe. This church, more like a small cathedral, is also worth a visit with its 300 foot-high tower, splendid vaulting, flying buttresses, and a dazzling interior of gilt and paint.

BRISTOL – SEVERN BEACH
by Owen Prosser

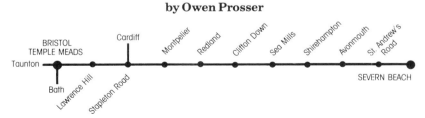

This line, currently marketed by British Rail as the 'City – Severn Line', offers a 13½-mile-long run from Temple Meads, the first two miles over the double-track route to South Wales and the North. This takes one to Narroways Junction, a few hundred yards beyond Stapleton Road, where the branch proper swings off to the left and follows a great curve on an embankment from which a wide sweep of the city may be seen in panorama fashion.

Two books have appeared on this line in recent years, both by well-known local transport historians, Messrs Colin Maggs and Mike Vincent; the latter's *Lines to Avonmouth* being the more recent. In them, one may learn of how the nucleus of the present route lay in the original one from Avonmouth to a terminus below the Clifton Suspension Bridge at Hotwells, part of which as early as 1922 met the fate since suffered by numbers of others: conversion to a road.

The branch as we find it now has several features worthy of note, the first being that it is not only Bristol's sole surviving local suburban service with, over its inner reaches, closely spaced halts taking passengers into and out of the city along its single track (double till the late 1960s), but also the only example of a line of this kind surviving in all the West Country.

We have to continue our run, according to the time of day in either a single-unit railcar or a DMU; call at the three inner city halts of Montpelier, Redland, and Clifton Down; and traverse the long tunnel of about 1-mile-length beyond the last-named to come face to face with the next striking feature. That is the outstanding scenery to be enjoyed as the train bursts out of Clifton Down Tunnel, which has taken the line from its urban surroundings of the usual back gardens to a position from which splendid views of the river Avon Gorge cutting through rocks and forests delight the eye from the carriage window. Nearly all large cities have their beauty-spots a certain distance away, and one cannot think of anything equal to the gorge so close to a built-up area and so easily reached.

This Avonside position has a stopping-place about half-way at Sea Mills, notable for the remains of an ancient dock originating in Roman times and for the display on the platform till recent years of a sign believed to be unique. It said that passengers should cross the line only by the subway, except when tidal conditions made this impossible – a reminder that, with a rise and fall of some 40 feet, the Severn tides (which affect the Avon) have the largest range in Britain and would flood the subway at its extremes. With single track replacing double, the notice became obsolete.

The railway track leaves the riverside at the Horseshoe Bend, sharply curved track following round a bend in the river so acute as to have led to the grounding of numbers of merchantmen when, till some twenty years ago, ocean-going ships used to sail down to Bristol Docks.

From the next stop, Shirehampton, a walk can be recommended to anyone who fancies a climb to a viewpoint, the top of Penpole Hill, from which there is a commanding view of the confluence of Avon and Severn and of Monmouthshire far away beyond the larger river. Another sight seen well from the summit is the combined road, cycleway, and footbridge carrying the M5 motorway over the Avon.

Resuming the train trip, a short run takes the passenger from Shirehampton to Avonmouth, the chief commercial and industrial centre served by the branch and, as the site of many closed sidings denotes, once a source of abundant freight traffic. The needs of industry led likewise to the building of the next station, St Andrew's Road, after which the character of the line changes for the final 3½ miles.

For this last stretch is, unlike that traversed so far, both level and almost entirely straight throughout. Although Severn Beach Station buildings were sold for other uses in October 1986, the walker who alights there has a pleasant stroll on offer. The swimming-pool, boating lake, and miniature railway that till the 1970s survived as mementoes of attempts in the inter-war years to exploit the Severnside position have gone, but there is still a sea-wall heading north and one can follow it to a point in easy reach of the road suspension bridge completed in 1966.

Apart from uniqueness in the job it does, alone of its kind in the West Country, and the views it offers in places, there is something else in which the Severn Beach branch is outstanding. This is the manner in which its more recent history demonstrates to perfection the value to BR of ideas put by, and given effect by, outside well-wishers. Timetable improvements made in 1964 to give an arrival time in Avonmouth better suited to those starting work at 9am trebled the numbers using a morning train and came from a passenger's suggestion. From the late 1970s, the Severn Beach Line Passenger Association has chartered many trains to provide excursions to places as far off as Brighton, Norwich, and Edinburgh, thus boosting the earnings of the branch by many thousands of pounds to the benefit of BR.

BRISTOL–BATH–WESTBURY
by Chris Phillips

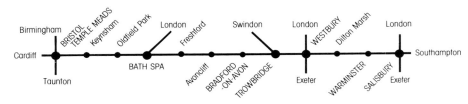

The 28-mile train journey from the ancient trading port of Bristol through to Westbury in the Wiltshire Downs involves traversing Brunel's incomparable main line to London for a distance of 15 miles.

Leaving the magnificent covered train shed at Temple Meads Station, our train threads right and heads due east. To the right, as we cross the River Avon, the modern diesel depot, where the fleet of 125mph vehicles are maintained, can be glimpsed at St Philip's Marsh. A red-stone cutting followed by two tunnels takes us into the valley of the Avon and on to Keynsham. To the left is the familiar landmark of Fry's (now Cadbury's) Chocolate factory, a main source of employment in this satellite town. There is another short tunnel before we reach Saltford, now sadly devoid of a railway station and so we are no longer given the opportunity to alight and enjoy riverside walks and rowing on the ever-present Avon.

Three miles farther on we enter the city of Bath through the grand Twerton Tunnel. The railway strides atop bridges right to the centre of Bath, thereby affording splendid views of this celebrated Roman and Georgian watering-place, before the train draws into the elegant and airy Bath Spa Station.

A modest walk from the station takes us up Manvers Street until, at the head of the street, we bear left at the traffic lights and proceed through North Parade and past Sally Lunn's – Bath's oldest building and now a tea-shop – to Abbey Green. This charming cobbled square is in the shadow, as its name suggests, of Bath Abbey, 'The Lantern of the West'. This stately edifice and the adjacent Roman baths are only ten minutes' walk from the station.

The Tourist Information Office is nearby, at 8 Abbey Churchyard (telephone 62831 or 60521). The visitor with more time will doubtless wish to call in there before exploring farther up the hill to the magnificent Georgian crescent, overlooking a pleasant park; and, on the way back to the station, rest in the riverside gardens and gaze on the unusual Pulteney Bridge. Other grand and interesting buildings worth a visit include the Assembly Rooms and the Museum of Costume.

The railway leaves Bath eastward with exceptional views of the city until Bathampton Junction looms and we bear right, sharing a wooded valley with the river and the Kennet and Avon Canal (now reopened), whose magnificent aqueducts span the line at Dundas near Limpley Stoke and at Avoncliffe. The small Wiltshire town of Bradford-on-Avon, with its tithe barn, Saxon church, and charming river bridge in the shadow of the mills that gave the place its prosperity, is well worth visiting.

Our continuing journey takes us on past Bradford Junction, where to the left the line through Melksham and on to Chippenham and Swindon (via the main line to London) bears away. This route was reopened to passenger trains in 1986.

Trowbridge, our next station stop, is a busy country town famed for the products of the local pie and sausage-makers (listen to the squealing across the station yard). It is also home to the county administration complex, and some time in 1987 a new railway station is expected to rise from the rubble of the dreadful state of affairs existing at the time off writing!

The final stop, Westbury, is a small market town lying in the shadow of the Salisbury Plain escarpment, upon which an imposing white horse is carved. The station is served by some High Speed Trains on the London—West of England route, although most pass by on the avoiding line. The route over which we have just travelled is served by an hourly Cardiff—Portsmouth link—due to be equipped with Sprinter diesel multiple-units in 1988—and some Bristol—Weymouth trains, though most of these start at Westbury. On the freight side, the scene is dominated by stone-aggregate traffic, which radiates from the Mendips—and has done so with ever-increasing tonnages for the past twenty years. On these profitable workings American-built Class 59 locomotives haul huge loads both east and south of this quiet Wiltshire town.

SALISBURY—WESTBURY
by Jon Honeysett

As a centre for rail-based tourists, Salisbury is perfectly sited, for in addition to the attractions of the city itself, the centre-piece being the magnificent cathedral with its 200-foot-high spire, it sits aside the main rail routes through Wessex. It is served by mainline expresses every two hours, from London and Southampton to Bristol and Exeter. During the summer, buses and coaches provide tours to Old Sarum and Stonehenge, from the main entrance of Salisbury Station, while for cyclists and pedestrians, quieter roads and lanes radiate out of the city, down the Avon Valley towards Fordingbridge or north on to Salisbury Plain.

To reach Warminster and Westbury, it is necessary to board a train to Bristol, composed at present of a locomotive hauling a five-coach set, but soon to be superseded by the new Class 150 Sprinter diesel multiple-units, with modern interior design, sound insulation, double-glazed windows, and air-conditioning.

The route from Salisbury to Westbury was originally a separate double-track line built by the Great Western Railway and running alongside the London & South Western double-track line as far as Wilton; but in the interests of operating economy the former GWR lines were slewed into the southern route just east of Wilton in 1968. The western route remains double to the present day, thanks to the heavy freight traffic, principally limestone aggregate, that uses it to reach the South Coast from the Merehead quarries in the Mendips.

Once clear of Wilton, the train plunges into the prehistoric heart of Wessex, running for the most part along the lovely valley of the River Wylye. These uplands of South Wiltshire must surely boast the highest number of Stone Age, Bronze Age, and pre-Roman fortifications in the British Isles, and all form 'ridge routes' liberally dotted with tumuli. The geological formations of chalk strata proved to be ideal defensive sites, particularly where intersected by streams and coombes, and to the south of the train can be seen the first of these 'castles' at Groveley, followed shortly after by Bilbury Rings and Stockton Earthwork. To the north are Stapleford and Yarnbury 'castles', complete with sheep grazing the downland turf, and interspersed with wonderful clumps of beech trees.

The Wylye Valley supports the usual mix of arable and dairy-herd farming, but the villages along the route are, unfortunately, now without their stations. Wilton North, Wishford, Wylye, Codford, and Heytesbury disappeared in the 1960s Beeching 'purge' – sadly so, for they would have made excellent starting-points for walkers and cyclists seeking the tranquillity of the flint-lined cottages and hamlets that typify the area.

This tranquillity, by a strange paradox, is the effect of Salisbury Plain being used as the British Army's main training ground since Boer War times. Indeed, there are species of butterfly, moth, bird, and flowering plant that owe their very existence to the 'machinery of war' which, when the wind is in the right direction, can be heard booming from the artillery ranges at Larkhill, and the tank training grounds at Tilshead.

The run without any station stops is a fast one, and the 20 miles from Salisbury to Warminster is reeled off in twenty-three minutes. Having passed Codbury Ring to the north of the train, our approach to Warminster is marked by the imposing summits of Scratchbury and Battlesbury camps, the latter being the 'jewel' of the hill-forts at 682 feet in height, and virtually inaccessible on its west and north-east faces because of the steepness of the incline.

Just as Salisbury Plain sees Challenger and Chieftain tanks 'slugging it out' in combat (albeit mock-combat), so the hills round Warminster echoed to the battle-cries of warriors in combat more than a thousand years ago when, from AD 871 to AD 897, King Alfred and his Wessex Saxons struggled to free the land from the Danes. How fitting, then, that Warminster should be headquarters of the No. 1 School of Infantry, and as our train draws into the town's station, it passes numerous barracks and workshops, served by rail sidings. Buses run from here to Longleat House, which is a big attraction for families wishing to see the beautiful gardens and the wildlife park, while the town itself, with a population of 16,000, retains the charm of a rural market meeting-place.

As the train leaves Warminster, the view to the west includes the strange conical Cley Hill, at 784 feet in height thought by many to be artificial, though there is no evidence to suggest this. If the weather is fine, the Mendips in Somerset can just be glimpsed before the train descends Upton Scudamore bank through Dilton Marsh Halt – a small wooden platform, just long enough to accommodate a single carriage, but obviously useful for the inhabitants of the hamlet close by.

Running down into Westbury, our route crosses the avoiding line built by the GWR in 1906 to speed the passage of its expresses from Paddington to Devon and Cornwall, and used today by its High Speed Train successors. Away to the north, the rim of the plain is marked by the famous White Horse, originally cut into the side of the chalk hillside near Bratton 'castle' to mark the site of Alfred's famous victory over the Danes in AD 897.

At Westbury's busy station we can change for trains to Weymouth, Penzance, or Swindon; or continue to Bath and Bristol over the route described on page 20.

SWANAGE

by Trevor Garrod

The resort of Swanage on the attractive Isle of Purbeck (actually a peninsula) was served by a branch line from Wareham until British Rail closed it in 1972. A rail-link bus service with through ticketing now runs from Wareham Station to Swanage along the busy

Swanage Railway train at Herston. (*Photo:* Trevor Garrod)

A351 road—but the line itself survives in two places.

Some 2½ miles of the track, from Worgret Junction to Furzebrook, is still in use for oil trains. The trackbed continues, with all bridges still in place, through Corfe Castle, whose dramatic ruin dominates a narrow gap in the Purbeck Hills, and over rolling farmland to Harman's Cross—whence track recommences for the final 3 miles into Swanage.

A campaign to preserve the line started when it was first threatened with closure; and since 1979, steam trains have again been run out of Swanage, by the Swanage Railway Company Limited. The company and its associated bodies own seven steam locomotives and a variety of passenger and freight stock, including a diesel shunter.

Swanage Station is in the town centre, handy for the beach and also serving as a bus station. During the tourist season, steam and some diesel trains run out into the Purbeck countryside. Until 1986, these terminated at Herston Halt, 1 mile away, from where walks up into the Purbeck Hills are easily made. But track was also laid farther west to Harman's Cross and trains are due to continue through to this village in 1987.

At present the Purbeck line, as it is usually now called, is a fairly modest one in comparison with some other preserved railways. It has a lot going for it, however, and deserves to succeed in its ultimate aim of a restored passenger service linking with such tourist sites as Corfe Castle and the Blue Pool at Furzebrook, and providing the 8,000 inhabitants of Swanage, as well as the many summer visitors, with a train connection to the rest of the BR network.

(For details of the railway company's services, and how to join its supporting association, write to Station House, Swanage, Dorset, BH19 1HB).

CASTLE CARY–YEOVIL–DORCHESTER
by John Penny

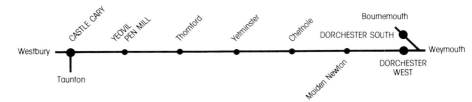

The junction station of Castle Cary is the start of our 32¼-mile trip on the singled line to Dorchester. Trains on this route start their journey at Westbury, or in a few cases Bristol, and run through to Weymouth.

There is now ample room to 'park and ride' at the much-improved Castle Cary Station. The main-line platforms have been lengthened, and we have to cross to the far side of the island platform to board the (more often than not) DMU which runs down to the coast.

The branch swings away from the main line, under a road bridge, and we soon realise how our route undulates. Even so, fast running can be made as we have no curves of note and often welded rail beneath us. Soon Sparkford Sawmills are noted on the left, sadly no longer rail-connected; the site of Sparkford Station – completely obliterated – and, as we dive under the A303 we see on the left the former creamery (also at one time rail-served) now part of the Haynes Publishing Group. The rise and fall of the line provides interest, as we view from the three car diesel set, and we pass, almost without discerning it, the site of Marston Magna Station. Soon we slow dramatically and swing to the right to see

Weymouth train at Yetminster. (*Photo:* Chris Burton)

our first stop—Yeovil Pen Mill—possibly passing an up train, about 12 miles and fifteen minutes from Castle Cary. A bus service links Pen Mill to the town's bus station and to Yeovil Junction Station on the Salisbury—Exeter main line.

To our left, as we stand in Pen Mill, we see one of Yeovil's links with the past—Pittard's Leather factory, which processes and sends skins far and wide. Yeovil's biggest single employer is, of course, Westland Helicopters, now firmly on the map after recent wranglings. A sprawling industrial estate adjacent to Westlands and named 'Lynx' after the 'chopper' follows the course of the old Yeovil—Taunton rail link, closed in 1964, and 3.6 miles of this line have been taken over by a new road as far as the A303 at Cartgate, Martock.

From Yeovil, easy access by road is possible to several sites of interest: Montacute House, Worldwide Butterflies (Compton House, on the Yeovil—Sherborne A30 road), and Sparkford Motor Museum, run as a trust by John Haynes. In addition there are local beauty-spots such as Ninesprings (within walking distance of the town centre), Flam Hill Country Park (Duchy of Cornwall land) and, adjacent to the ex-L&SWR main line, Sutton Bingham Reservoir, a haven for sailors and fishermen.

From Pen Mill (where we notice that semaphore signals still abound), it appears that the line has doubled—but as we swing round in a long arc, the up line diverges in the direction of Yeovil Junction, and though it sees no scheduled passenger services it is quite often used as part of a diversionary route. We pass under the main line at right angles, soon to halt briefly at Thornford, ignoring the nearby sewage works.

We are now climbing into hillier country and, a mile farther, we stop at Yetminster. There is no sign now of the sidings which once hosted an array of banking engines to push trains up the fearsome Evershot bank. Our DMU works harder now, but our climb is interrupted for after 2 miles we stop at Chetnole Halt, then climb onwards for 2 more miles before plunging into the first of the line's three tunnels, slightly curving to the left as we leave and taking a quick look at the sparse remnants of Evershot Station.

Down the bank we go, having crossed the watershed and reached the valley of the River Frome. Note the attractive balustrade of the overbridge leading to Chantmarle House, now a police training college. It's drifting all the way as we pass the village of Cattistock (which also once had a halt) on the left and then the brakes are applied, bringing us to a stand in the station of the sleepy country town of Maiden Newton, all but 25 miles from Cary and in forty-four minutes.

Like the village stations farther north, Maiden Newton is a useful railhead for walkers and cyclists exploring the Dorset Downs; and it is also on the West Dorset Cycleway, the leaflet for which gives a variety of combinations for rides out to Lyme Regis, up to Sherborne, and down to Dorchester. This station was also the junction for the Bridport branch, closed in 1975, and has a loop line where we may pass an up train.

Since descending Evershot bank we have crossed and recrossed the River Frome, and as we leave Maiden Newton and run round the hillside the river can be seen again, much bigger now, as we enjoy the Dorset lanscape. We plunge into another tunnel, also taking us under the A37 which is glimpsed from a viaduct as we pick up speed from the tunnel's mouth. We exchange various hand signals with traffic on the road before crossing it, adjacent to the disused concrete platform of Stratton Halt, again crossing the River Frome, which remains in view and is recrossed twice more, whilst our embankment affords us a fine view of the river valley until we disappear into the blackness of Dorchester Tunnel.

After a sharp swing to the right we emerge to the outskirts of Dorchester itself, the line becomes double and we enter Dorchester West Station, at the time of writing a disgraceful sight to behold with boarded-up windows and graffiti—a sad shadow of its past. Let us hope that someone will take some action on this station—for experiences elsewhere have shown that an unstaffed station need not be an eyesore.

Despite the appearance of its West Station, Dorchester, just under an hour's journey from Castle Cary, is an attractive town to visit and is described on page 15. A few minutes' walk brings you to the modern South Station, for trains to Bournemouth; or you can continue on this train to Weymouth (see page 15).

WEST SOMERSET RAILWAY
by Alan Harwood

The resort of Minehead, the 'Gateway to Exmoor', is a very popular destination for day visitors and holiday-makers alike, but unfortunately British Rail withdrew the Taunton–Minehead passenger service after 2 January 1971. However, the desire for reopening it as a private railway was inevitable, and following protracted negotiations involving BR, Somerset County Council, and the embryo West Somerset Railway, BR sold the Minehead branch line to the County Council in July 1975 for £245,000. The Council then leased the line to the WSR to allow the gradual reopening from Minehead to Norton Fitzwarren–in reverse order to the building of the route between 1857 and 1874–in two stages, Norton Fitzwarren–Watchet and Watchet–Minehead.

Events since 1975 have vindicated the Council's action, and the combination of luck, timing, and persistence has ensured survival. Initially, the Minehead–Blue Anchor section was reopened on 28 March 1976, followed by successive sections to Bishop's Lydeard by 9 June 1979. This 19¾-mile section has ten passenger stations, with occasional shuttles on the additional 2¾-mile Bishop's Lydeard–Norton Fitzwarren section, up to Taunton Cider's premises. The beautiful and varied scenery traversed is a recommendation to travel Britain's longest private railway, especially on diesel railcars.

In 1983, Taunton Cider acquired by lease part of the Minehead branch line as a freight siding up to the junction with BR at Silk Mills crossing. Track rationalisation in 1986 caused resiting of the junction ½ mile west. Happily, a direct connection on to BR from the WSR via Taunton Cider's siding remains, thus safeguarding the ultimate aim of trains into Taunton, tentatively from 1988. Uniquely, the WSR will not terminate adjacent to Taunton BR Station, as the Minehead branch starts 2 miles west at Norton Fitzwarren. The ramifications of this feature has created a knot of problems affecting the WSR, BR, and the National Union of Railwaymen, so far unravelled, but probably capable of solution.

Thus, at Taunton one catches the WSR's bus link at either Station Road or outside the station travel centre. A preserved maroon and grey Bristol Lodekka bus generally covers the 5 miles, passing Taunton School playing fields and Norton Manor Commando Camp *en route* through Taunton Deane farmland to Bishop's Lydeard Station, off the A358 Bypass.

Bishop's Lydeard is a large village nestling peacefully in the Quantock foothills, the fine fourteenth-century Parish Church of St Mary the Virgin having a sandstone tower. The Bell Inn, within its shadow, produces Bell Bitter real ale. The down platform station building, of about 1862, comprises booking office, waiting room, and toilets, being virtually identical to that at Williton, and sporting the traditional Great Western Railway colours of light and dark stone. The goods shed, now extended as a carriage workshop, adjoins a Nissen-type building housing the Taunton Model Railway Group (open to the public on certain summer Sundays). The nearby railway cottages, listed as

Crowcombe, West Somerset Railway. (*Photo:* Walter Harris)

Buildings of Special Architectural Interest, are now converted into a farmhouse. The elaborate bargeboards are also a feature of the railway buildings, like the former Station Master's house, opposite the hipped-roof GWR signal-box.

The Norton-Fitzwarren – Bishop's Lydeard section occasionally carries trains on gala days. It became double track under the GWR's Minehead branch expansion scheme in the 1930s. Usually, however, diesel railcars and diesel and steam trains start from the up platform at Bishop's Lydeard and run to Minehead, as does the 'Quantock Belle' dining train.

To the right of the line, beyond Bishop's Lydeard Station, notice both the prominent parish church tower and Cedar Falls Health Farm. The latter is visible amid wooded parkland as the sinuous line climbs Crowcombe summit. Past more woodland, the line twice crosses the A358 at Combe Florey. On the left, Combe Florey manor house, home of the writer and critic Auberon Waugh, is glimpsed, then the rendered and thatched Farmers' Arms Inn. On the right, the steep western flanks of the Quantock Hills loom in the distance, running parallel to the line, to end abruptly at St Audrey's Bay, east of Watchet. Combes and rolling farmland pass by and the line enters a deep sandstone cutting, both cutting and gradient diminishing as the summit is breasted at Crowcombe Station.

This station, in idyllic sylvan surroundings, is a good base for Quantock country walks for which *Walks in the Quantocks* (Merlin Press, Spaxton, Somerset, 1984) is recommended. Bicycles and rucksacks are commonplace with Crowcombe Youth Hostel nearby and both preservation and working facets of this railway are apparent.

An unusual attraction at this restored and award-winning station is the down platform trackwork display, depicting the evolution of railway track from the broad-gauge era of 1860 till today. This permanent display was a WSR contribution to the 1985 festival 'Great Western Railway 150'. Restoration of Crowcombe passing loop is planned, with trains serving both platforms under the control of a new GWR-pattern signal-box and associated semaphore signalling.

The train now begins a leisurely descent to Williton. To the right is Puff Cottage, the former Crowcombe Station Master's house, with elaborate bargeboards, noticed just before the road overbridge. Then, turning eyes sharp right, the outlines of Triscombe Quarry are seen before the line curves between beeches and conifers, opening out into rolling land and passing two automatic open level crossings. The Tower folly of Willett Hill, in Willett Wood, can be spotted distantly on the left.

Stogumber Station, with a single two-coach platform, the line's smallest, soon appears. The former goods shed and yard, beyond the stone building, is an attractive picnic area. The village, ¾-mile west, stages in August an annual music festival. As the descent continues, narrow combes on the Quantocks' escarpment, with open moorland above, are intermittently visible. Bicknoller village, nestling at the foot, is revealed as open country unfolds, with Sampford Brett and the distant Brendon Hills beyond passed on the other side.

Williton Station, ½-mile from the village, has two bi-directional platforms, a water-tower, and the only surviving Bristol & Exeter Railway signal-box. By the level crossing is the noted maze garden of Highbridge House, well worth seeing. The widely spaced platforms are evidence of former broad-gauge tracks. Notice that the former GWR lower quadrant signals fall into the 'off' position; other railway companies' signals usually rose to indicate 'off'.

Williton is a good centre for walks on the Quantocks and to Nether Stowey, finishing at Crowcombe Station or vice versa. The pre-war village fire brigade achieved a notoriety when it was immortalised in the Will Hay film comedy *Where's That Fire?*

The Diesel & Electric Group's depot next to Williton down platform is passed and the line follows open country as far as Doniford Beach Halt. It then skirts the coastline, here unsuccessfully invaded by the Danes in 988, Doniford Holiday Camp being glimpsed and, visibility permitting, South Wales, too. Soon we have a vista of Watchet harbour and the distant mass of Minehead's North Hill, just before arriving at the one-time terminus of Watchet.

This small town is Somerset's only commercial seaport, as occupied quays and berthed ships show. Occasional pleasure-boats on Bristol Channel cruises also call to be met by boat trains. The harbour was immortalised in Coleridge's *Rime of the Ancient Mariner*, written at his nearby Nether Stowey home, now the National Trust property of Coleridge Cottage. Watchet Museum, a distinctive building on the charming main street is also worth visiting.

Climbing out of Watchet, the line passes Wansborough paper-mills on the left, overlooked by St Decuman's Tower. After a girder bridge, the trackbed of the West Somerset Mineral Railway, closed in 1911, runs left alongside towards Washford where a grass mound bordering the village playing-field veers inland to the Brendon Hills; the trackbed is now a footpath between Watchet and Washford. The masts of Washford BBC Radio transmitting station appear.

Washford Station bears green enamel signs heralding the headquarters of the Somerset & Dorset Railway Trust, dedicated to the memory of the Somerset & Dorset Joint Railway. The station building houses an interesting museum (open Sundays and Bank Holidays from Easter to September) with the restored Midford signal-box on the platform, and sidings here hold the SDRT collection of historic railway vehicles. Historic Cleeve Abbey is easily reached from the station while the WMSR trackbed can be traced alongside the Washford River to Roadwater, beyond which a road reaches Comberow, the foot of the Brendon Hill Incline.

Our line descends Washford bank revealing a panorama of the Brendon Hills on the left, Old Cleeve village and Chapel Cleeve Manor on the right. Beyond a caravan park the coastline reappears and we reach the crossing-point of Blue Anchor Station.

The hamlet of Blue Anchor is a good base for a low-tide beach walk to Minehead. Despite the inviting sands, locals avoid bathing in the doubtful waters of Blue Anchor Bay, but new outfall treatment works may change this. The seafront road is a good viewpoint for Conygar Tower, above Dunster, and the dramatic bulk of Minehead's North Hill. *Aficionados* of 'Great Westernry' should visit Blue Anchor Museum on the down platform.

Blue Anchor Station has a unique wheel-operated level crossing by the GWR signal-box, after which the line skirts the seashore, the inland side being a backdrop of wooded hills. Dunster Castle belonging to the National Trust, dating from the Norman Conquest, and latterly the Luttrell family home, stands ¾-mile from the station, dominating the village. At one end of the wide main street stands the Yarn Market, the Castle dominating the other end, with rendered terraced buildings on each side selling local souvenirs and offering tourist facilities. The Castle and its grounds are open seasonally to the public. Below the ramparts, on Mill Lane, is Dunster water-mill, an original seventeenth century working mill (open April–October) that sells stone-ground whole-wheat flour.

One can also reach Dunster Beach from the station, then turning left along a coastal path bordering Minehead Golf Club, ending at the promenade by Somerwest World, formerly Butlin's Holiday Camp, whose facilities appeal to active visitors.

The line now crosses Dunster Marsh, giving a good view of Conygar Tower and verdant slopes of the backdrop of Exmoor Hills, crossed by many well-trodden paths and tracks. Somerwest World appears on the right, the seashore reappears and Minehead terminus is reached. The spacious island platform boasts a large canopy dating from the GWR's 1930s station rebuilding, and there is a good railway shop and buffet.

Minehead, the main town of West Somerset, derives its name from the old British word 'mynydd', meaning hill, due to the dominating bulk of North Hill, in the Exmoor National Park. Its summit offers glorious vistas across the Bristol Channel, Blue Anchor Bay, and the distant Quantocks. The long-distance Somerset and North Devon Coastal Path starts on Quay Street below North Hill, and sheltering under the hill is the fishing-boat and pleasure-craft haven of Minehead Harbour. It lost its pier through Second World War anti-invasion measures, so the local council enforces special berthing arrangements for calls by the PS *Waverley* and the MV *Balmoral* on the revived Bristol Channel pleasure cruises.

The Parish Church of St Michael, on the slopes of North Hill, is sometimes floodlit and can be reached by climbing Church Steps between the thatched and rendered Higher Town Cottages. These contrast with the imposing slate-roofed Victorian and Edwardian buildings along the tree-lined Avenue between the seafront and the shopping centre. A helpful Tourist Information Centre is at Market House, The Parade (telephone 0643–2624). Inside are displayed 1950s era BR posters promoting Minehead as a holiday resort. Now the town is a centre for the delightful Exmoor and North Devon area, worth discovering on foot, by cycle, car, or coach.

The whole railway is normally open between Easter and October, with all-year Saturday Williton–Minehead diesel railcar services, plus December Santa specials. For train services write to West Somerset Railway, The Railway Station, Minehead, Somerset TA24 5BG or telephone 4996. Inquire for details of BR/WSR combined day tickets from Western Region stations.

(The author is indebted for permission to quote from the *West Somerset Railway Guide* (West Somerset Books Ltd, 1986) in the writing of this article).

EXETER – EXMOUTH
by Joan Fuller

City of Exeter

Visitors to the City of Exeter will enjoy seeing the Guildhall, the oldest municipal building in the country, rebuilt in 1330; the Cathedral, which had its first bishop, Leofric, enthroned by Edward the Confessor in 1050, and other reminders of its ancient past. The Exeter Heritage Project provides free guided tours from the Cathedral and the Quay (see here the Maritime Museum), during the summer months. But Exeter is also a modern city, with a variety of department stores, shopping precincts, and a brand new Plaza Leisure Centre, close by St Thomas Station.

To leave Exeter for the coast at Exmouth, there is a choice of two main stations, Central and St Davids. St Davids Station served by all trains travelling to Plymouth and westwards to Penzance, is the busier, and most trains to Exmouth start from here. It is within a few hundred yards of the latest covered precincts – the Guildhall shopping area and the Harlequin shopping complex. This is the station largely used by the commuters from Exmouth and beyond.

The service is provided by Skipper diesel multiple-units, the name thought by British Rail to be appropriate for the West Country. Trains run at half-hourly intervals on weekdays and hourly on Sundays, the latter subject to some curtailment during the winter. Some of the Exmouth trains start at Paignton or Barnstaple and, although these are very limited, it does enable the traveller to avoid changing trains at Exeter.

The journey from Exeter to Exmouth from St Davids with the Skipper screeching its way round a sharp bend to tackle the 1-in-36 bank of the fifty-chain connection between St Davids and Central Station. This piece of line was opened in 1862, to link the London & South Western Railway and the Great Western Railway. The Skipper manages the climb and goes through the short Bank Tunnel to emerge at Central Station.

A few years ago, Exeter Central suffered from a run-down, neglected look, but nowadays it appears quite bright. Former waiting rooms and offices have been let to commercial enterprises, their entrances blocked on the station side, which gives a tidy overall appearance. A new waiting-room has been added on one of the adequately sized platforms.

Tall iron railings are still standing which used to separate Fyffes' banana warehouse from the rail-traveller but now one can only peer through at the less exotic cement company. Beyond this yard on the north side of the station stands Exeter's prison, an ugly red-brick building.

To the south, however, there are glimpses of the elevated Rougemont Gardens. The Rougemont area has an interesting history; it was from here that Exonians made a stand against William the Conqueror in 1068. The gardens, on the site of the former castle, are within two minutes of the High Street and certainly worth a stroll beside the dried-out remains of a deep moat, through the old city walls to the grounds where the main War Memorial for Exeter's dead in two world wars is situated. The view northwards across the city is extensive, towards some of the University buildings and the hills beyond.

Exeter Central Station has a recently reopened entrance/exit at the east end, which takes the traveller into the junction of High Street with Sidwell Street, this providing a nearer approach to the higher end of the shopping centre. The main station entrance, in

Queen Street, houses a travel centre which sells tickets and provides information and brochures.

Exmouth Branch

After leaving Exeter Central, if ours is a stopping train, within two minutes it will arrive in a deep cutting at St James' Park, called 'Lion's Halt' until 1946. Exeter City football ground is beside this halt. The main stand can be seen if one looks upwards towards the south – a green corrugated-iron structure. The allotments on the north side look more attractive, especially during the summer. Allotments are a feature of this branch line, and many are cultivated quite intensively.

Leaving St James' Park, the train goes through the Blackboy Tunnel and emerges into a very built-up area. On the north side are the newer post-war houses; on the south side the closely built terraces of the early twentieth century. None of the housing encroaches on the railway, for once again allotments, a brickyard, and a road keep them quite separate. Our line begins to turn south-east off the main Waterloo line, and remnants of the heyday of the Southern Railway can be seen. This area was known as 'Exmouth Junction' and extensive buildings and marshalling yards covered a vast area. Fifty years ago, a small child was most impressed by the sight of the huge locomotives being fired ready for their next turn of duty. In those days, off-duty train-driver fathers, were inclined to take their offspring for a very rare treat to the engine sheds on a Sunday morning.

Exmouth Junction was a carriage and motive power depot. The concrete works produced fence posts, platform slabs, and other concrete furnishings for the Southern Railway. Some of the concrete constructions of engine sheds and workshops are still used as part of a coal depot. The rest of this vast area is now a shopping centre and petrol station.

It has taken the train three minutes to travel from St James' Park to Polsloe Bridge Halt, where the line becomes single track. The singled track leaves one long concrete platform on concrete pillars quite unused. The small ticket office-cum-shelter on the unused platform has been attacked by vandals, but Southern Railway concrete structures and fences are made to withstand vandalism. The long platforms accommodated full-length trains which would stop here while ignoring smaller halts.

The train leaves Polsloe Bridge, the gradient falling then rising at 1-in-150 into a cutting under a road bridge on its way through the village of Whipton, over main roads until it approaches the Sowton industrial estate to the west of the line. There are proposals to build a halt at Sowton, and a local BR Manager has said that, if it is built, all daytime trains will stop there. This should be popular with the industrial site owners and their customers, and users of the nearby M5 motorway service area.

A longer ride of eight minutes enables the train to speed on to Topsham. The first hint of water is seen here as boat-building yards begin to proliferate. The level crossing on the approach to the station is at present operated by the signalman from his manually operated box, soon to be replaced by automatic signalling. The station retains its roomy platforms but has lost its wooden superstructure. The Station Master's house, designed by Sir William Tite, is currently up for sale. It does not, perhaps, have the appeal of a small country station master's house, but it should fulfil somebody's fantasy – although there would be little time to indulge this with ghostly imaginings, as trains run on this line from approximately 6.30 a.m. until 11.30 p.m.

It is worth breaking your journey at Topsham. This ancient port on the River Exe has an interesting history. It was largely built to accommodate traders who exported wool to the Low Countries in the seventeenth and eighteenth centuries. Some of the older houses on the Strand show the influence of Dutch architecture; the bricks for them quite often came from Holland, having been brought back in the holds of ships as ballast. The wharf once had a rail siding, where ships discharged cargoes of coal, timber, slate, and stone for

Exeter city, but the trackbed has now become a road.

There is a strong sailing community in Topsham with a flourishing yacht club. It is possible to sit outside, on a clear day, at one of Topsham's good inns and enjoy your food and drink while taking in a view across the Exe to Haldon Forest. Alternatively you can sit in the churchyard of the Parish Church of St Margarets and enjoy a more elevated view.

The line now follows the shore after crossing the five-span River Clyst Viaduct, originally constructed to take a planned double track to Exmouth which was not built. Exton Station, renamed from Woodbury Road in 1958, is three minutes from Topsham and 6 miles from Exeter. At high tide, the water laps the embankment to the west, but to the east the station building offers comfort. Nearby, the Clyst runs into the River Exe and swans ride the water with their young during the summer.

In due season, the Exe Estuary has a wide variety of bird life. Avocets, greenshanks, redshanks, cormorants, oyster-catchers, and sandpipers make the area a great attraction for the serious and not-so-serious ornithologist. At low tide, the scene is very different. The mud extends practically the whole distance from one side of the estuary to the other, except for narrow channels of water, but the feeling of space and distance and the openness of the aspect is still very beautiful.

Soon after Exton, to the east of the railway, the Lympstone Marine Commando training centre stands out as stolid square white buildings which house the marines and the administration offices, while nearer the line are their terrifyingly difficult assault courses. The halt Lympstone Commando, opened in 1976, is used exclusively for authorised persons travelling to and from the camp.

From Lympstone Commando, we glimpse to the east an attractive house and gardens with lily ponds, called 'Nutwell Court'. These grounds are very occasionally open to the public in aid of charity. New owners are replanting the garden with shrubs and trees. The property is in a beautiful setting and worth a visit if possible.

The river bank is now slightly to the west of the track as the train approaches Lympstone Station, 9 miles from Exeter. The village is sited between two red promontories on the banks of the Exe and faces, across the river, the parklands of Powderham Castle, home of the Earl of Devon. Lympstone dates back at least to Saxon times, owing its prosperity to fishing and agriculture and to it being a small port. Only a few fishermen operate from the village now. Salmon is netted in season and shellfish are gathered from the shore, and lugworms at low tide – the silhouettes of bent banks seen far out across the mud.

Lympstone's small foreshore is very popular with artists. It is possible to sit here, at all but the highest tides, and have a view across the estuary to Powderham Castle, framed by large deciduous trees. With a good pair of glasses one can look back to Exeter, the Cathedral standing out from the background of hills. Look to the west at Exminster, with its imposing hospital, soon to disappear, to Starcross and the Brunel Atmospheric Railway building and on to Dawlish Warren. The area nearest Exmouth was always known as 'Exmouth Warren' and some forty or fifty years ago there were many holiday bungalows built mostly of wood, but they gradually disappeared. The journey from the Exmouth dock area, in a small rowing-boat, to the warren was always a hair-raising experience. Nowadays a motor-boat taxi does the trip far more comfortably.

From Lympstone, the train runs over a three-arch viaduct across the village and follows the slight curve westwards to the point at Exmouth some 1½ miles away. The view across the estuary can be quite breath-taking, as the eye moves on from sailing-boats on the river to the woods on the far side and the great Haldon Hills.

The last four-minute lap beside the River Exe brings us into Exmouth Station. The present Exmouth railway station is the third. The first operated from two private houses when the line opened in 1861. In 1924, the Southern Railway's purpose-built red-brick station was a four-bay two-storey structure, whose imposing forecourt had lampposts on piers. This building was demolished in 1975 to make way for a bus station. The British Rail station, now consisting of a small ticket office and single platform, is slightly to the north of the 1924 building. The new combined road and rail station was opened in 1980. When Devon County Council cut their subsidy, Devon stopped most of their buses short of the station.

Exmouth

This town is Devon's oldest seaside resort. It became popular in the eighteenth century, both with Exeter people and those from farther afield. The Beacon was a very fashionable area on high rising ground with such famous visitors as Lady Nelson and Lady Byron.

Today there are 2 miles of sandy beaches as well as other beaches beyond the eastern end of the promenade. The entertainments on the beach, mostly to attract and amuse children, are not intrusive. During the summer there are numerous river, sea, and canal trips, as well as mackerel-fishing on offer.

A walk to the western end of the beach brings the visitor to the docks. Exmouth is quite a busy small port and it is intriguing to watch fairly large cargo boats being expertly manoeuvred, with literally inches to spare, into the harbour.

The passenger ferry to Starcross, from the ferry steps at the docks, runs from May to September. From Starcross it is possible to return by train to Exeter or walk along the west bank of the River Exe and the Exeter Canal. By travelling in the opposite direction, one could go by rail from Starcross to Dawlish, Teignmouth, and beyond.

There are other walks over the cliffs to Budleigh Salterton and even to Sidmouth. The Exeter Information Bureau, Manor Gardens, Alexandra Terrace (telephone Exmouth 263744) is open from Easter to the end of October. It has a wealth of information about walks, houses, museums, excursions, and the Exmouth Leisure Centre, but the beach – given good weather – may well be all the visitor will need.

EXETER–BARNSTAPLE

by Ian Dinmore

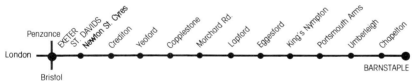

This railway is the longest branch line in the West of England and is famed for its beautiful scenery as the line winds its 39 miles from Exeter to Barnstaple, the capital of North Devon.

On leaving Exeter St Davids, the train travels for a short distance on the main line towards Paddington until the branch diverges at Cowley Bridge Junction. Here on the left may be seen a small waterfall which forms part of the River Exe flood-defence system.

The first station is Newton St Cyres, with this pretty Devon village just a short walk from the station. Here also is the Beer Engine pub right outside the station, which brews its own beer on the premises. The next station along the line is Crediton, the home of St Boniface with a beautiful Early English church built in the local red sandstone.

Shortly after leaving Crediton, the train passes over a minor road and the crossing has

Barnstaple – Exeter train approaches Lapford. (*Photo:* Rod Muncey)

the delightful name of Salmon Pool Crossing. The line here appears to be double track, but the left-hand track is for freight trains only. Yeoford, the next station, was once the junction for trains to Plymouth via Okehampton. After Yeoford, the left-hand line turns off towards Meldon Quarry, which is a prime source of railway ballast.

In recent years, some excursion trains have used this freight-only line as far as Okehampton, on the edge of the Dartmoor National Park. The route from Meldon to Bere Alston has been lifted, but the final section of this former London & South Western Railway main line to Plymouth is still in use and is described on page 00.

Just beyond Yeoford on the left look out for the picturesque village of Coleford with its many thatched cottages. The train travels on to Copplestone, the highest point on the line and about 300 feet above sea-level. At this point we are also at the watershed between those rivers and streams flowing southwards into the English Channel, and those whose waters flow northwards into the Bristol Channel. Our train calls at Morchard Road, the station for Morchard Bishop, 2 miles away, and then we come to Lapford Station, the only other place on the branch that has goods trains. These are handled in the small and efficient goods yard on the left, where grain and fertiliser are brought in and timber sent out.

Just after Lapford we pass under Nymet Bridge and on the left see the confluence of the River Yeo and the famous River Taw which is noted for its salmon. We now enter the beautiful Taw Vale with away to the left the foothills of Dartmoor and on the right Eggesford Forest. This area is the true heart of Devon, unspoilt by the commercialism of the South and hardly touched by man.

The next station is Eggesford – 'The Ford of the Eagles', although there is no village of that name. This station serves both Chulmleigh and Chawleigh about 3 miles away and is very popular with fishermen. Just before you arrive at Eggesford, look out for the charming little church on the left. This is the now-disused Church of All Saints and to miss visiting this beautiful historic building would be a crime.

Eggesford is a crossing-point for trains on the line, and is about half-way between

Exeter and Barnstaple. I would most strongly recommend alighting here for a short while; either for a walk up to the church, which is always open, and a visit to the nearby garden centre with its nursery and café, or for a short stroll to the Fox and Hounds Hotel, which is just 400 yards from the station and is situated in its own large grounds on the bank of the Taw. Here you can partake of some of its excellent cuisine or make use of its renowned accommodation. There are also many walks through Eggesford Forest. During the summer months the rhododendrons line both sides of the railway here and afford a spectacular scene best viewed from the train.

We now leave Eggesford and, still following the river, look out for herons, hawks, and deer, this area being abundant in wildlife. Kings Nympton, the next station, once served the small town of South Molton, 8 miles away, and is still the railhead for a host of smaller villages near by. There is also a small hotel, The Fortescue Arms, here, which is ideal if you are on a fishing holiday.

Three miles further on is the small station of Portsmouth Arms. As at Eggesford it is not named after a village but after the adjacent pub, the nearest village being Burrington about 3 miles distant. The railway twists and turns as it follows the passage of the River Taw before reaching Umberleigh, best known for its beautiful station gardens and frequently awarded the trophy for the best-kept station on the line.

The penultimate station is Chapelton, just over 4 miles from Barnstaple. Here on the left are Chapelton sawmills. If, when you are out for a walk in North Devon, you have to cross a gate, this is where it is most likely to have come from. After leaving Chapelton, and on the final approach to Barnstaple, look out on the left for a strange-looking building and church. The building is St Michael's School and the church is the parish church of Tawstock.

We cross the River Taw for the last time and our train soon draws into the station at Barnstaple. There is much to see and do in this town of 17,000 people; but your journey need not end here, for most trains connect with a bus that leaves from just outside the station entrance for the popular seaside resort of Ilfracombe. From the bus station in the town (just a short walk across the bridge from the railway station) you can also take buses to Lynton, Bideford, Croyde Bay, and many other resorts.

Barnstaple has ten trains a day, but only three on Sunday, the fastest taking just under an hour from Exeter. For further information call in at the Information Office at Barnstaple Station, where the staff are always more than willing to help you plan your journey; or you can telephone Barnstaple (0271) 45991. For tourist information in North Devon, telephone (0271) 72742 and for details of bus services telephone Barnstaple 45444.

EXETER–TORQUAY–PLYMOUTH
by Fiona West

If you have travelled to Exeter by InterCity 125 from Paddington or Bristol, you will find that the train does not go quite so fast beyond Exeter St Davids – but this gives you more time to enjoy some remarkable scenery.

Soon after leaving Exeter St Davids we pass through the city's third station, St Thomas

35

which like the next two is served by local trains to Paignton. We are in open country before long, and passing under the motorway bridge we presently reach the shore of the Exe Estuary with Powderham Castle just on the right.

At the next little station, Starcross, there is a ferry across to Exmouth, operated by Mr R Rackley, of Dawlish (telephone 0626–363540). Also at Starcross is a monument to one of Isambard Kingdom Brunel's less fortunate projects – the Atmospheric Railway. The idea was to pull trains along by attaching them to a pipe, laid between the rails, through which air was sucked. This ingenious form of traction was used between Exeter and Newton Abbot in the 1840s, but was not too successful. Nowadays you can still visit Brunel's pumping-house alongside the line here at Starcross to see a working model of the railway, an exhibition and an audio-visual show. It's open every day – for details write to The Old Pumping-House, Starcross, Exeter, or telephone 0626–890000.

The sandy bar at the mouth of the river is served by Dawlish Warren Station, after which there is little between our train and the open sea – just narrow strip of beach. Brunel built the line on a sea-wall at the foot of the cliffs, and has thus given us a ride that must be unique in Britain. The small resort of Dawlish is somehow tucked into a gap in the great red cliffs and its houses and hotels overlooking the stream and the Lawn make a pretty picture.

By the River Teign. (*Photo:* Sean Gamage)

We then continue this memorable seaside run through five short tunnels, interspersed with picturesque coves, before turning inland through a deep rock cutting behind the town of Teignmouth – quite an old town and a pleasant resort.

Now the scenery changes as we run alongside another estuary, that of the River Teign and inland to Newton Abbot – a fair-sized town of 20,000 people. Notice the race-track on the right before we curve left into the station of what was once an important railway town. Line closures have made it less of a major junction, but you can still change here for Torquay and Paignton.

These two resorts are at the end of an 8-mile branch from Newton Abbot. They have a local service from Exeter but also some through trains from London, the Midlands, and the North. The branch leaves the main line at Aller Junction, just south of Newton Abbot, and passes the sizeable village of Kingskerswell, which used to have a station and

perhaps ought to have one again. It soon reaches the outskirts of Torquay and the train calls first at Torre, an unstaffed station serving the original village from which the resort took its name. Soon after we reach Torquay Station, very close to the beach and Torre Abbey.

Torquay with all its suburbs, has a population of over 100,000. Napoleon was brought here when it was only a village, and liked it; so did a lot of English officers, who brought their families here and the place soon grew into a fashionable health resort. Its mild climate and subtropical vegetation have helped build its reputation as one of our leading seaside resorts.

Torre Abbey, in beautiful grounds close to the station, is one of the oldest buildings in the town. It used to be owned by the Carey family, who transformed it into a mansion. It was bought by Torquay Corporation in 1930 and now contains an art gallery.

There is always plenty to do in Torquay. You can bathe on one of the sandy beaches; stroll among the lush gardens overlooking the sea, sail from the harbour and, if the weather happens to be bad, there is the Aqualand aquarium and the Coral Island Leisure Centre.

The train continues to Paignton, another resort adjoining Torquay, with sandy beaches and attractive greens, parks, and gardens. The train used to continue southwards from here to Kingswear; but that section, following its closure by British Rail, has now been taken over by Torbay & Dartmouth Steam Railway, which is described on page 38.

Back at Newton Abbot, the rest of the main line to Plymouth twists its way over and round the foothills of Dartmoor, through quiet Devon countryside with only one station, Totnes, still open. This small town on the River Dart is a charming place. There is a narrow, picturesque high street leading up from the river, with four old gates, an impressive red-sandstone parish church, a lovely old guildhall and, at the top of the town, the remains of a castle on a mound.

Totnes, with a population of some 6,000 has some good hotels and inns and is an attractive centre for touring this part of Devon. You can go by steam train up the Dart Valley to Buckfastleigh (see page 40) or, in the other direction, by river steamer for 10 miles down the ever-widening River Dart to Dartmouth.

The railway continues its curving course west of Totnes, up towards the summit at Wrangaton. At South Brent, the A38 trunk road appears on the left and runs close to the line for several miles. South Brent and Ivybridge, a few miles farther on, are both sizeable

Plymouth Hoe and Smeaton's Tower from the Citadel. (*Photo:* Roy J. Westlake, A.R.P.S.)

villages where a reopened station might be justified – but in fact, there are no further stops until Plymouth.

Our first sight of this city of 240,000 people comes as we run down the valley into the suburb of Plympton. Laira locomotive depot is passed on the left, and the line follows the Sutton harbour-side for a while before plunging into Mutley Tunnel; emerging from it for the final approach to Plymouth's modernised station.

TORBAY & DARTMOUTH RAILWAY
by Richard Jones

The Dart Valley Light Railway Company purchased the line from Paignton to Kingswear from British Rail in the autumn of 1972, there being no break between the end of BR services and the start of DVLR trains. Regular steam trains began operating over the line the following year.

The line was built in several stages from the main junction at Newton Abbot, reaching Paignton in August 1859. The section from Paignton southwards proved far more difficult to construct, with severe gradients, several viaducts, and a short tunnel. The line to Brixham Road (Churston) opened in March 1861, followed by the last section to Kingswear in August 1864. The station at Kingswear was connected to Dartmouth – on the opposite bank of the River Dart – by ferry. A further short branch, from Churston to Brixham, was opened in 1868.

The line was initially operated by the South Devon Railway, the GWR assuming ownership in 1876. Like the Ashburton branch, the line was converted from broad to standard gauge in May 1892.

Although having a local service from Exeter and Newton Abbot, the line was regarded as part of an important main line since it carried a good service of express passenger trains, including The Torbay Express to London. In contrast to the Ashburton branch, the line was firmly up to main-line standards and able to carry the largest and heaviest locomotives.

The inevitable decline of the line began in the 1950s. The Brixham branch was closed in May 1963, and all goods traffic ceased the following month. Steam services ceased in 1964, by which time the line was little more than a 'basic railway' operated by DMUs in the main. British Rail services finally ended in October 1972.

The T & DR has the most direct route between Paignton and Dartmouth, taking it along some of the most spectacular coastal scenery in South Devon and over the hills down to the Dart Estuary at Kingswear.

The journey begins at Paignton. The T & DR station is sandwiched between Queens Park (after which it is named) and the BR station. The station was built new by the DVLR in 1972-73 and incorporates the customary passenger facilities. A two-road shed adjacent to the platform is where the locomotives are based.

Soon after leaving Paignton trains pass over Sands Road level crossing, controlled by BR's Paignton South signal-box. For a short distance until the first stop at Goodrington Sands the T & DR runs parallel with the BR line to their carriage sidings at Goodrington. This section of line is still actually owned by BR. Goodrington Sands is a relatively modern station, with two platforms (one of which is not used) and the station building on the adjacent road bridge.

After Goodrington the line climbs steeply and soon hugs the cliff-tops round Saltern Cove, before passing over two viaducts, turning inland, and approaching Churston Station, the summit of the line. There is a passing loop here, controlled by a signal-box on the down platform, and a turntable in the station yard.

From Churston the line runs downhill, passing Galmpton village and through Greenway Tunnel, before approaching a further viaduct. After sweeping through woodland, the train gives superb views of the River Dart. The down gradient ends about a mile or so before Kingswear, where the railway runs beside the edge of the river

Approaching Kingswear. (*Photo:* Tom Heavyside)

Torbay Steam Railway, by the River Dart. (*Photo:* Tom Heavyside)

estuary, before arriving at the southerly terminus. Dartmouth can be clearly seen across the river, including the Royal Naval College.

Like the DVR, train services normally commence at Easter, and run daily from Spring Bank Holiday to mid-September; trains also run on selected dates in the early and late season. (For full details of services on the DVLR telephone Buckfastleigh 42338.)

The DVLR's larger steam locomotives are normally responsible for operating the line — including former 4-6-0 express engines and the larger tanks — in view of the steep gradients and heavy trains. Coaching stock has also been repainted in former GWR colours, and a former Pullman observation car is regularly attached to the train, offering unrivalled views of the surrounding scenery.

While the DVLR employs a nucleus of full-time staff to operate the line (as it does also on the DVR) volunteers from both Torbay & Dartmouth Railway Society and the Dart Valley Railway Association play a very vital supporting role in many capacities.

DART VALLEY RAILWAY
by Richard Jones

TOTNES ●―――――― STAVERTON BRIDGE ●―――――― BUCKFASTLEIGH ●

The branch line from Totnes to Ashburton was built during the 1870s and opened to traffic on 1 May 1872, worked originally by the South Devon Railway and later, from 1876, by the Great Western Railway. The line was originally built to the GWR's broad-gauge specifications, but converted to standard guage in 1892. The line was a typical Great Western country branch, operated by small tank engines and one- or two-coach passenger trains, shuttling to and fro to connect at Totnes with the main-line trains between London, Plymouth and Penzance.

The line began to decline after the Second World War. Passenger services ceased in November 1958; goods traffic lingered on for a further four years, but the last train ran on 7 September 1962. The branch had lasted ninety years.

Efforts to preserve the line and reopen it as a holiday attraction started soon after, and by 1965 volunteers had begun the long, uphill task of restoring the 9½-mile branch to its former glory. Their considerable efforts were rewarded on 5 April 1969, when the first public passenger train for eleven years ran between Buckfastleigh and Totnes. On 21 May 1969 the line was officially reopened by Dr Richard Beeching.

Since Easter 1985, Dart Valley steam trains have been able to operate into and out of the BR station at Totnes. The station is situated on the main line between Newton Abbot and Plymouth, a little over 222 miles from London Paddington, via Bristol. It is a two-platform station with four tracks – two through roads and two platform roads. Most of the sidings have disappeared in recent years. A new station building has been built relatively recently, though the old GWR canopies remain in excellent condition. The signal-box and old Brunel Atmospheric Railway pumping station stand adjacent to the up platform.

Soon after leaving Totnes Station northwards the line passes over the River Dart. Immediately after the bridge is Ashburton Junction, where the Dart Valley branch begins proper. On the left is Totnes Riverside Station, together with passing loop, for many years the southerly terminus for DVR trains. The DVR Association is currently constructing a 'new' station here in keeping with GWR tradition, which has involved the rebuilding of a genuine timber station building.

The line follows the course of the River Dart all the way to Buckfastleigh. On its way to Staverton – now the only intermediate station – the line passes two Water Aurhority

Dart Valley Railway near Staverton Bridge. (*Photo:* Tom Heavyside)

pumping stations, the grounds of Dartington Hall, Staverton village (about a mile from the station), Nappers Crossing, and the historic Staverton Bridge over the river.

Staverton is one of those tiny, timeless country stations which are a joy to behold. Situated in a very picturesque part of the valley, the station boasts a level crossing and signal-box, and a former GWR camping coach is normally resident in the bay platform. The station has running water, but no electricity.

After passing the former Staverton Station Master's house, the line continues to Buckfastleigh, 7 miles from Totnes and—since 1971—the northern terminus of the DVR (the Buckfastleigh—Ashburton stretch was 'lost' when the new A38 road was built). Buckfastleigh was once a thriving town, but many of the local industries have declined since the 1950s.

The station at Buckfastleigh has changed significantly in recent years—from a typical large GWR country station to becoming the headquarters of the DVLR Company, complete with new sidings, workshop, engine sheds, and ten acres of riverside grounds forming a 'leisure park'.

Train services normally commence at Easter, then run on selected dates in April/May. Trains run on most days from the Spring Bank Holiday, throughout the summer until mid September. (For full details of services telephone Buckfastleigh 42338.)

Trains are hauled by a variety of former GWR tank engines—normally 45XX 'prairie' tanks, 14XX 0−4−2 tanks, and 16XX/64XX pannier tanks. A few industrial tank locomotives are also normally available for service. As the DVR's main workshop is at Buckfastleigh, a number of larger engines can also be viewed, which are undergoing restoration/repair before use on the Torbay & Dartmouth Railway. The coaching stock is repainted in the former GWR colours of chocolate and cream.

The line is actively supported by theDart Valley Railway Association. Membership brings unrivalled benefits including excellent free travel concessions on both Dart Valley lines, a quarterly journal *Bulliver,* and the opportunity to work on the line in a variety of capacities. Full details can be obtained from: DVRA Membership, The Station, Buckfastleigh, Devon TQ11 0DZ.

CITY OF PLYMOUTH
by Phoebe Lean

Plymouth? Oh yes, of course, the Hoe and the Devonport Dockyard!

But first, from the station turn right over the highway footbridge, to take a No.1 or No.2 Hoppa minibus (every seven minutes)—to the Loyal and Ancient Borough of Saltash reached in a quarter of an hour. We cross the Tamar into Cornwall by the 2,107-foot long road bridge which twenty-five years ago replaced the steam chain ferry at this centuries-old best crossing-point and was opened for the owners, Plymouth Corporation and Cornwall County, by the Queen Mother. This first suspension bridge since London's Chelsea Bridge—spanning 1,100 feet, standing 135 feet above high water, and with its twin towers 240 feet above piers of Cornish granite—became the prototype for the Forth, Severn, and Lisbon bridges, and the world's longest Humber Bridge.

Alongside strides the Royal Albert Bridge, Brunel's masterpiece of 1859, its unique double tubular arches bearing InterCity 125 expresses at a restrictive 15mph into the adjacent Saltash unmanned station, below the Norman parish church. Or you could take a train.

'Saltash was a borough town when Plymouth was a furzy down,' and still possesses on parchment her second charter of AD 1190 (the date of the first is unknown). Her two magnificent 3-foot−6-inch silver maces dating from 1746 are unique in displaying crossed oars above the crown, to confirm ownership of the water and ships' dues from

Tamar's Weir Head round Devonport and Plymouth to the River Plym; which right was sold to the Admiralty in 1898. King William III wanted to site the naval dockyard at Saltash, but the burghers said it would spoil the oyster-beds and salmon-fishing. Halfway down the hillside is the stone cottage of Mary Newman, Drake's first wife.

If you return to Plymouth by Hoppa from Fore Street bus stop, first glance round at the mouth of the ¼-mile tunnel being built for the trunk road Saltash By-pass before going on to alight in the city centre at Royal Parade. This area was disastrously blitzed in 1941, but already in 1943 rebuilding plans were drawn, and in 1945 construction began of four parallel main shopping streets. A red building intact and conspicuous among the wilderness of ruins, still houses the *Western Morning News in New* George Street.

Look now across Royal Parade. First from the top roundabout with the new fountain, honouring Plymouth's twinning with the Polish port of Gdynia, you see St Andrew's Parish Church, gutted in 1941 by fire but, labelled 'Resurgam' (I shall rise again), providing open-air services until restored in 1957. Next stands the Guildhall, likewise gutted and damaged but now carefully reconstructed. The new windows depict local history, such as the arrival of Henry VIII's Katherine of Aragon, while round the main hall's ceiling are the Labours of Hercules signifying effort and determination.

Cross by the underpass, and after a glance to right at the grim brown edifice of the new Theatre Royal, without fail make for the municipal complex with its tower block. The Information Desk just inside supplies a handy map and essential guidance for your further exploration of the city.

This broad thoroughfare, Armada Way, is the main approach to the Hoe. The great Anchor came from HMS *Ark Royal*. On the right notice the small Catholic church, placed usefully for daily entry since their cathedral, with its tall slender spire, is now not very central. On the left is the Holiday Inn, one of the city's several high-class hotels among a varied selection of accommodation, that also includes the YMCA, YWCA, a Youth Hostel (occupying an 1823 banker's house with cupola and pillars), and the Salvation Army which here posseses two bands.

There is, of course, a bowling-green, though not at the point where Drake continued his famous game – really because the weather pinned his fleet in old Sutton Pool. Proceed to the great Naval War memorial, where four lions guard 7147 and Neptune guards 15,575 Plymouth-based names lost at sea. Then look at Drake, bold with hands on globe and sword (here most respected then for, when Mayor, bringing Dartmoor water to his citizen mariners and merchants); also at the Britannia Armada memorial bordered by guns and balls, and further back the obelisk to the German War.

From the Hoe's wide expanse you see Rennie's mile-long breakwater, completed after twenty-eight years of struggle in 1840 to provide safe anchorage. At the east end is an iron pillar and ladder to an iron basket, refuge in wild storms when the angry waves sweep even over the huge wide wall. At the west end is the harbour light and, in the centre, a free-standing fort, now used for abseiling. Fourteen miles out to the south-west, perceive Douglass' lighthouse on the menacing Eddystone reef, now capped with helicopter pad and the two-seconds-every-ten-seconds blink, now automatic. Beside you stands Smeeton's earlier lighthouse, removed in 1882 from a weakening part of the rock (where its stump can still be seen) and now a fine land-mark.

The close-in island is Drake's Island, once used as a prison, He had it fortified, saying, 'Whoever holds the island, holds Plymouth.' It is now an adventure centre for many sports, the barracks a multi-national hostel.

You may see a warship rounding the buoys of the winding deep water to the Hamoaze, the 8-mile dockyard stretch of the Tamar; or a swift ferry from Roscoff or Santander, berthing in the commercial Millbay Docks at the corner. There the transatlantic liners passed their clientèle by tenders from or to the mail trains on the quay lines, the level crossing and city viaduct linking Paddington directly in four hours. You may dine now in their two restaurant cars at the Great Western Society's Didcot steam preservation centre.

Notice below you the sea-water swimming-pool and the high dive; the pier was blitzed. The marine biology aquarium on your left is second only to London Zoo's. Above looms the star-shaped Fortress Citadel, built by Charles II not only against invasion but also pointing some guns towards the Cromwellian city. Guided tours lead you by the splendid entrance arch, round the walls and views and into the lovely St Catherine's Chapel.

A half-hourly launch trip from nearby Phoenix Wharf will in three-quarters of an hour speed you to the naval dockyards, the largest in Europe, with her captain pointing out the Scott Memorial (he was a choirboy here) and King William, and specifying each warship that happens to be in dock or alongside, the buildings, structures, submarines (some nuclear), and on its four legs the most powerful of naval cranes. The twin ferries on their chains ply to Torpoint; the lower Cremyll ferry for foot passengers enables you to reach Mount Edgcumbe house and park on Cornwall side.

On your return, visit the West Pier for the Mayflower Stone, and tablets commemorating Captain Cook, the Tolpuddle Martyrs, and other historic events. On the Island House, read the list of Pilgrim Fathers (and Mothers). You are now in the old fishing port, the Barbican and Sutton Pool, with industrial sites on the Plym River. Your Information Guide and Map will conduct you round some of the city's treasures: the Elizabethan and other Tudor houses, the old Gin Distillery and seventeenth century Debtors' Prison, and even the Jewish Merchants' Synagogue, second oldest in Britain.

Then head for Bretonside bus station, and above it the skeleton Charles Church, memorial to the Blitz. Find a No.20 bus for a quarter of an hour's ride out to the Plym Valley Railway at Coypool Road stop—the fine achievement in steam preservation by reconstruction of a piece of the ex-GWR line over the moors to Princetown. Besides six South West locomotives, you can inspect and clamber up *Springbok*, a three-articulated Beyer-Garrett from South Africa, now the largest locomotive in Europe. In October 1986, the Minister for Transport came to inspect the voluntary PVR membership at track-laying and to open the expanding site.

On your return to the city, what about visiting the Polytechnic with marine speciality, the College of St Mark and St John from Fulham, the comprehensive museum, library, art galleries, the Barbican antiques market and, next to it Cap'n Jasper's Tea Bar, reputed to brew the best cup of tea in the world! Indeed, what about spending a very protracted weekend in the historical diversity of Plymouth?

PLYMOUTH—GUNNISLAKE
by Clive Charlton

There are few railway branches left like the Gunnislake line. From the middle of a big city you can set off on a thoroughly rural ride that leads into the heart of one of Britain's most scenic and fascinating river valleys. The Tamar's mining and industrial past has faded back into the landscape over the years, but has left many clues that can be well seen from the train window, with more to be discovered from the stations venturing on foot with a map. The journey itself is quite an event, with a change of direction half-way, steep inclines, sharp bends, and all the delights of the 'Low Speed Train.'

For the first few miles from Plymouth Station, the train follows the former Great Western main line to Cornwall out through the city's undulating suburbs, and calls at the few survivors of a once-numerous set of local stations. First comes Devonport, where the long, bare platform suggests busier days. Then beyond a short tunnel, the more modest Dockyard Halt heralds a view from the viaduct over the extensive naval repair yards that line the Tamar to the west of the railway. On the opposite side of the line, Late Victorian terraces built to house dockyard workers march rhythmically up the steep hillside.

After Keyham, where some of the station buildings are still intact, there is another view of the dockyard complex from the viaduct crossing Camel's Head Creek. The very large crane marks the site of the nuclear submarine depot.

From a brief halt at the signal on the viaduct, the train passes over to the up line before entering the branch itself at St Budeaux. This also marks a move from ex-Great Western territory to that of the Southern system, for the section from St Bordeaux up to Bere Alston was opened in 1890 as part of the London & South Western Railway's independent main line into Plymouth from Waterloo, via Exeter and Okehampton. The line from St Budeaux into the city centre closed in 1964, and much of the route has been obliterated.

The single-line token is retrieved from its box on the platform at St Budeaux and the train sets out as the sole occupant of the branch. Soon there is a stirring close-up, of the two great bridges over the Tamar to Saltash, with Brunel's magnificent wrought-iron spans of 1859 alongside the 1961 road suspension bridge. Then comes a rather exuberant gallop right alongside the river, past the sinister sprawl of the Royal Naval Armament Depot on the right, reinforced concrete, dull huts, tunnels in the hillside, and undoubtedly a large quantity of high explosive. The recently installed sidings generate the branch line's only freight traffic.

At high tide, the train skims along, only a few feet from the water's edge; at low tide, there are waders and sea-birds on the mud – gulls, dunlin, redshank and sometimes, a solitary curlew or heron on motionless watch.

After a brief burst of speed, the brakes go on, for the train has to creep over the bridge across the mouth of an arm of the estuary, Tamerton Lake. There is a speed restriction here to limit further deterioration of the bridge. On the other side is the closed Tamerton Foliot Station, now used as an education centre for an adjacent nature reserve in Warleigh Wood.

The next water crossing is altogether more ambitious – the long iron viaduct over the Tavy, depressingly rusty but evidently still in essentially sound condition. Infinite combinations of tide and weather mean the broad reaches where the Tavy meets the Tamar always look different. On a still, misty autumn morning at the turn of the high tide, it can be some enchanted, silent lake. If a south-westerly gale is blowing, you are reminded that this is after all an arm of the sea, with steel-grey waves pushing up river. Then at low tide, the fascination is in the patterns on the glistening mud. Looking up the Tavy to the right where distant wooded hillsides lead the eye right up on to Dartmoor, Great Mis Tor and Staple Tor stand out on a clear day.

The Tavy Viaduct takes the railway to the nose of the Bere Peninsula and immediately the train begins a steady climb. Before the Tamar is hidden from sight, the waterfront village of Cargreen appears, huddled on the Cornwall bank. Earlier in this century, the locals could take a ferry boat over the river here and walk across the fields to catch the train at Bere Ferrers Station, which is now the first stop beyond St Budeaux. Passenger accommodation at Bere Ferrers is nowadays a most unglamourous concrete box, but the station still has some dignity. The old station house and waiting room have been sold privately and fitted up with authentic British Railway signs of the 1950s. 'Ladies Room', 'Way Out', 'Passengers Must Cross The Line By The Footbridge' – never mind if there is no footbridge or that the signs are in the orange of the North Eastern Region, rather than Southern green – it is a welcome touch of colour.

The waterside village of Bere Ferrers is largely out of sight, but the old village core, with its quay and interesting church is worth a visit. The mud-flats on the adjacent River Tavy are the haunt of wintering avocets.

From Bere Ferrers, the line threads the heart of the Bere Peninsula, with only occasional glimpses of the Tamar shining in the distance. The train climbs steadily all the way through a private landscape reserved for the railway passengers and the farmers – steep slopes under bracken, thick woods and pasture. Deep cuttings in slate rock and sturdy embankments are reminders that this stretch was engineered in Late Victorian times to carry the main-line trains of the LSWR, although the path of the second track is now disappearing under a tangle of vegetation. Near the top of the climb, the land falls away to the left to reveal a grand reach of the Tamar stretching away to a small group of buildings on the Cornwall bank. This is Halton, remote now, but once a busy quay serving the farms and mines inland from the river. Above the distant bend in the Tamar rises the parkland of the Pentillie estate. A curve to the right brings the train into Bere Alston Station. Here, the driver changes ends, while the guard walks down the platform to pull on the points lever.

Compared with the Spartan simplicity on the rest of the line, Bere Alston still clings to some fragments of its former status as a junction station. Not only is there the mechanical ritual of changing the points, but the original platform canopy, with splendid ornate iron supports, and an abandoned island platform opposite, complete with signal-box, waiting-room, and the piers and steps of the footbridge. But there are no trucks loading flowers in the goods yard now, no green express going on to Tavistock, Salisbury, Woking, and Waterloo. The gorse grows thicker on the old trackbed beyond the buffer stops at Bere Alston; twenty-five years ago, *Eddystone, Watersmeet* and *Sir Trafford Leigh-Mallory* struggled to restart their trains up there, but the Beeching axe was permanent. It is sadly futile to wonder if Plymouth-bound commuters might more sensibly ride to work from Tavistock by train, rather than roar down the A386 in Sierra and Golf.

In the old days, you changed into the branch train at Bere Alston – all stations to Callington – but now it is simply a change of direction as the careful descent to Calstock begins. From here on, the journey is on a railway line that never aspired to be anything more than a local service, built for access rather than speed. The bends are tighter, the slopes are steeper. It is one of Britain's more bucolic railway rides.

If you are up in front, you can watch the driver twitching the brake handle to check the speed as the train creaks and grinds down a narrow rock cutting. Then comes another glorious view of the Tamar below, with close-nurtured strips of horticultural land below Bohetherick on the Cornwall side falling steeply to reed-fringed marsh pasture by the river. The sheltered slopes of the Tamar Valley once made its fruit and flowers as celebrated as its mining industry. Much of this has passed into legend – the clouds of of cherry blossom on the hillsides, acres of strawberries, railway wagonloads of double-white narcissi leaving for distant markets... Imports, energy and labour costs have extinguished much of the valley's horticulture, but from the train you can still see patches of orchard, branches gnarled and wreathed in lichen, and there are plenty of good, fresh Calstock tomatoes in Plymouth market in the season.

As the river passes briefly out of sight, the far bank is cloaked in thick woods, hiding the medieval walls of Cotehele House and its gardens. Shortly afterwards, the Tamar makes a sharp right turn, and the railway follows it round still creeping downhill, with the rather elegant balconies of the Danescombe Valley Hotel glimpsed at the angle of the river bend. Then comes the Gunnislake line's *tour de force,* the *other* great railway bridge over into Cornwall – the Calstock Viaduct. You have to decide which side to look out – a frustrating choice, for there is rather too much to see. Besides the wider views of the Tamar in its sinuous course through the hills, there are many details lingering from the river's commercial past. To the left down on the Cornwall bank are the former quays, once served by the East Cornwall Mineral Railway, a tramway that brought copper ore, bricks, and granite from Gunnislake and beyond for shipment that brought in seagoing vessels and Tamar barges. The stone for Dover Harbour, Blackfriars Bridge, and paving for the streets of London went out from here, while coal, timber, and limestone were landed, the latter for burning in the limekilns still visible alongside the river. The lime they produced, together with rich and ripe street sweepings brought up from Victorian Plymouth, helped keep the Tamar Valley soils very productive. The tramway reached the quays via a steep, cable-worked inclined plane, its course now hard to detect without a map.

Upstream of the viaduct, there is an aerial view of the roofs of Calstock tumbling in grey, angled abandon towards the river's edge. Down beyond the landing-stage, where pleasure-boats come in summer, were once piled the batches of copper ore awaiting shipment to the refineries of Swansea and Neath: now it is children playing and trippers watching the tide ebb past. On the opposite bank of the river the solid and solitary farm used to be the Passage Inn, with tea-gardens and swings and a foot-ferry over to Calstock. On the sloping land between the farm and the viaduct are two decrepit tin sheds. At the turn of the century, when Calstock Viaduct was being built, there was a shipyard on that land. It takes particular imagination to believe that not only rowing-boats and Tamar barges, but even seagoing sailing-ships were built there. The last large vessel built was the ketch *Garlandstone*, launched in 1909, and miraculously still afloat at Porthmadog, North Wales.

There is much of interest for those who choose to get off at Calstock and explore with the aid of a map. The town centre still has a strong old-fashioned flavour from the busy days of the nineteenth century, when Calstock was a booming and doubtless brawling place that attracted hundreds of miners and their families. Visitors are catered for today with several pubs and restaurants although Calstock has so far escaped the mass tourism that afflicts the more popular of Cornwall's coastal villages. The network of local lanes and footpaths offers a range of interesting routes for the walker. Particularly recommended is the walk west along the river to the National Trust's Cotehele properties.

From Calstock Station the line climbs steeply above the town. Looking back at the splendid grey viaduct, it is almost disappointing to learn it is made of concrete blocks rather than local stone. Then horticulture, dead and alive again; overgrown fields, broken glasshouses but also new plastic tunnels for lettuces and tomatoes. They still grow fruit and vegetables on the smallholdings across on the Devon side of the river, although the woods hide decaying orchards as well as mines that produced lead and silver. Farther up river, there was a brickworks and the copper- and arsenic-mines of Gawton, whose poisoned mine dumps still scar the hillside. The crooked chimney on the crest of the wooded slope pumped out fumes from an arsenic refinery. Pollution is no recent invention!

After ½-mile of eastward travel, the train crawls back round the hillside. We are treated to some truly rustic railway. First we stagger to a halt. Up here, far from the high-speed InterCity, the *train* stops at the level crossings. With a ritual toot on the horn, it cautiously restarts up another narrow rocky cutting into the woods, with time to study the vegetation alongside. Look through the trees to the right for the old river port of Morwellham away down in the valley. The leaves, branches, and ferns crowd in closer. It is a big disappointment *not* to arrive in triumph in the heart of a fairy grotto. In fact, the view that opens to the north is magnificent, with Gunnislake visible beyond the steep, thick woods and the cliffs of Morwell Rocks. Perhaps the Victorian promoters of river trips may be forgiven for calling the Tamar Valley the 'Devon Rhine'.

After another stop at a level-crossing, here are more reminders of the Victorian copper-mines. On the left are the ivy-covered chimney-stacks and engine-houses of the Calstock Consols Mine and nearing Gunnislake, more ruins and mine dumps, gorse and heather grown, where Drakewalls Mine produced copper and some tin. The whole landscape springs from the mining past – the straggling settlements and even the small fields, for sometimes the miners ran smallholdings on the side.

The last ½-mile to Gunnislake is actually the oldest part of the whole route from St Budeaux. This is because the existing line joins the courses of the earlier East Cornwall Mineral Railway of 1872 coming up from Calstock Quay. Despite its antique character, the section from Bere Alston to here cannot even pass as Victorian. A latecomer on the railway scene, it was completed in 1908, but it did attempt to compensate for this retarded start by opening under the imposing title of Plymouth, Devonport & South Western Junction Railway! The fleet of three tank engines that chugged up here for decades had names. Two were noble – *Earl of Mount Edgcumbe* and *Lord St Levan*, and one more plebeian – *A. S. Harris*.

Now high above the river, out of sight down in the valley, the train reaches the present terminus; which is perched some way up the road from Gunnislake village. Until closure in 1966, the upper end of the line continued on as far as Callington Station, sited a mile north of the town at Kelly Bray. There are currently plans to relocate Gunnislake Station to the south side of the main road, to permit demolition of the rail overbridge, with its limited headroom.

For now, the Gunnislake branch is said to be safe from closure. It survived the Beeching cuts of the 1960s because road access from Plymouth to the communities it serves is extremely poor. The very landscape that makes it so attractive has helped preserve it. Although the journey is there as a much underrated delight for Plymothians and visitors, it is a basic part of life for many people living in the Tamar Valley. The early morning train takes workers to the Dockyard. Later come the commuters to offices, banks, schools, and colleges. In the middle of the day, pensioners and mums with toddlers go to the shops or town. They would be hard-pressed without the train. On Saturdays and holidays, children ride down, thinking more of the bright lights of Plymouth than old mine chimneys. If ever British Rail see salvation in sweeping minor details like the Gunnislake line from their network, it will be a cruel day for the locals, and an experience missed for the many who have no idea it exists.

PLYMOUTH – PENZANCE
by Noel Sloman

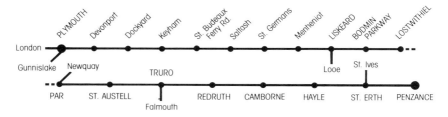

Main-line trains to Cornwall share the line west of Plymouth Station with the local service to Gunnislake (decribed on page 00). After the junction at St Budeaux, a left-hand curve enables the passenger to view Brunel's great Royal Albert Bridge before the train slows to a crawl to cross it. The engineer's name is proudly emblazoned on the face of the tower.

After passing Saltash (described on page 42), the train continues to curve left, thus affording further backward views of the two great bridges over the Tamar and forward views of the Hamoaze, the seaward end of the river, and Devonport Dockyard with its perpetual stock of mothballed warships.

That the train is now in Cornwall is obvious. The route is tortuous with scarcely a couple of hundred yards of straight track. The gradients are considerable and valleys are crossed by enormous viaducts. These viaducts were originally wooden trestles on stone piers in true Brunel fashion, but when age decreed they should be replaced, the new was built alongside the old and the line slewed on to a new alignment. Many old pillars were left standing and can be seen covered with foliage alongside the new viaduct.

A good example is at the first major stop in the Duchy, Liskeard, junction for the Looe branch. Moorswater Viaduct crosses the route of the old Looe, Liskeard & Caradon Railway, of which the present Looe branch is a remnant, and is about ½-mile west of Liskeard Station.

A little farther on, ruins of Doublebois Station lie beside the track. This station served Dobwalls, which can be reached by bus from Liskeard. A good walk from the village is the 7¼-inch gauge Forest Railway, which features some superb American outline locomotives, including a 4−8−8−4 Mallet-type Big Boy. There is also a fascinating display of famous bird paintings of Thorburn in a unique setting.

From Doublebois and its lineside rhododendrons, the route plunges into the Glynn Valley, crossing on its way a very slender viaduct. The track has been singled and sand-drags are incorporated in case a train overruns the stop signal at the top.

Bodmin Parkway, renamed from Bodmin Road in 1985, is near the bottom of the valley. Here is the junction leading to Bodmin General and the historic Bodmin & Wadebridge line. Alas, Wadebridge is no longer rail-connected, though there are buses to it from here; and the line from Parkway to Bodmin General is still intact. The private Bodmin & Wenford Railway Company hopes to have steam trains running between the two stations in 1987. They are negotiating to buy Bodmin General to Boscarne Junction, whence ran the mineral line to Wenford Bridge, the third steam railway ever built. It is hoped eventually to operate this line with narrow-gauge trains, as the road bed is too lightly laid for standard-gauge passenger trains. Modern signalling made Bodmin Road signal-box redundant, and it is now a tea shop run by a railway enthusiast.

Lanhydrock House, a National Trust Property, lies just north of the line, but little remains of the private station provided for the Robartes family by the GWR. A few miles farther on, on an escarpment on the up side, is Restormel Castle, once the home of the Black Prince, now owned by English Heritage. It is accessible, though a very good walk, from Lostwithiel, next station down.

Lostwithiel was once a wooden station in the Brunel style but has been rebuilt by BR. Unlike the Portakabin style of Bodmin Road, the new buildings at Lostwithiel are very attractive. The same cannot be said for the monstrosity overshadowing them. St Ivel creamery, just on the up side of the level crossing, is a perfect example of a functional building being made as overpowering as it is possible to do. Lostwithiel is a very ancient town and will repay a stop. The branch of Fowey, closed to passengers, heads away on the down side, carrying only English China Clays' traffic.

The main line now sweeps south to Par, where the harbour is entirely dedicated to the shipment of china clay. The white dust that pervades everywhere does nothing to enhance the view.

The line is now in china clay country, and sundry sidings on the up side run some miles up into the 'Cornish Alps', the massive white spoil tips which disfigure this part of the country. Some effort has been made to 'beautify' some of the older tips by planting them

with rough grass and grazing them with Soay sheep (which apparently need little or no shepherding), but with only moderate success. Nothing can be done about the current tips, on which white waste is poured in vast quantities day and night.

St Austell with a population of 25,000, is the next stop, and the Norman church here is worth leaving the train to see. The Market House opposite is of interest though strongly modernised. The china clay company has been made to filter out much of the waste, and the White River in the valley no longer justifies its name. For the same reason, the beaches around St Austell Bay are greatly improved.

From St Austell ran the peculiar 2-foot-gauge Pentewan Railway. Traces can still be found and at Pentewan can be seen the great dock that was built to compete with Par and Charlestown. Unfortunately it receives the full force of easterly gales and sailing-ships were often marooned in the dock waiting for the wind to change. Silting was a great problem and the dock company and railway folded.

The bus ride from St Austell to Mevagissey is picturesque, as is the village of Mevagissey itself. Although overrun by holiday-makers in July and August, it is still very much a fishing port with a considerable fleet. There is also an extremely good model railway in one of the fish cellars with a collection of over 1,000 locomotives on display besides the operating layout. It is the owner's proud boast that he has a model of every class of GWR standard-gauge locomotive plus a few broad-gauge ones; most of the Southern and a goodly number of LMS and LNER. British Rail locos are also represented as are some American ones with peculiar wheel arrangements.

Between St Austell and the county town, Truro, were several small stations all now demolished. Despite a public outcry, BR insisted on singling the track to save maintenance costs. Pray that your train is not late or it will be held at the single-track section, thus fulfilling the prophesies of the complainers.

Truro is approached over two great viaducts, both offering superb views of the city and its cathedral. This small city of 15,000 people certainly justifies leaving the train for exploration. As is so often the case, the station is the best part of a mile from the centre, but a frequent service of Hoppa minibuses will take you down the hill. The County Museum is worth a visit if only to gaze in awe at the 5-inch-gauge model of *City of Truro* the original being the first vehicle in the world, not just the first locomotive, to top 100mph. There is also an excellent model of the sole GWR Pacific engine, *Great Bear*. Models of mines and mine engines, displays of minerals and crystals, and an excellent art gallery can take up at least half a day.

Cornwall came under the See of Exeter until 1870, when the Truro bishopric was restored after a lapse of 800 years. St Mary's Parish Church was partly demolished, the south aisle remaining, and the cathedral built on the site. It was the first cathedral to be built in Britain for over 300 years and the last one to be built in stone in the Gothic style.

Some terrible constructions have defaced the main streets. The 1930s Plaza Cinema despoils the otherwise elegant Georgian Lemon Street, as does the sheepskin shop on the corner of Boscawen Street. Fortunately the planners have now seen sense, and developers have to retain at least the facade of the old buildings and thus retain the original aspect of the streets. One of the last coasting paddle-steamers, the *Compton Castle*, lies in a basin – it has been cleverly converted to a restaurant.

The train leaves Truro through Higher Town Tunnel and immediately afterwards the Falmouth line (described on page 58) turns away south. On the same side can be seen the earthworks of the original route from West Cornwall to the riverside wharf at Newham, closed to passengers when the present main line arrived from Plymouth in 1862 and to

Opposite: Class 50 locomotive heads down the lush valley to Lostwithiel with a Liverpool – Penzance train. (*Photo:* Rod Muncey)

goods traffic in the late 1960s.

Chacewater, once junction for the Perranporth and Newquay branch, has vanished, but some earthworks on the up side remain to show where the branch was. Derelict mine engine-houses and their chimneys abound here, memorials to a past industrial age. It is hard to imagine that some villages hereabouts were busy towns when Manchester was little more than a village.

The line is still tortuous and a great sweep leads into Redruth. Station Hill is aptly named. The London end of Redruth Station is in a deep cutting, the Penzance end out on a viaduct. Despite all the efforts of Redruth's shopkeepers, it is not a very attractive town. It clambers up a hill steeper even than Station Hill. In one cottage lived William Murdoch, the inventor, and it became the first home in the world to be lit by coal gas.

The surrounding area, scarred as it is with old mine workings, is much more interesting. The County Council have a programme of capping the dangerous shafts and the number capped is nearing 3,000. Some of the shafts have been colonised by horseshoe bats, an endangered species, and caps have had to be specially designed to allow the bats easy access but to keep the humans out!

Between Redruth and Camborne can be seen several sets of pithead gear. Some serve South Crofty Mine, threatened by the disastrous 1985 fall in tin prices. With reluctant Government help, the mine continues to operate. Two others at East Pool, owned by the National Trust, are open to visitors from April to October and are impressive relics of the industry. A frequent bus service between Redruth and Camborne runs past one and within a ¼-mile of the other.

For the visitor who stays on the train there are panoramic views away to the sea on the up side. On the down is Carn Brea, a huge hill crowned with an Iron Age fort. Carn Brea Castle, said to date from the fourteenth century, is an excellent restaurant.

Camborne is where Richard Trevithick, pioneer of high-pressure steam and 'Father of the Locomotive', was born and worked. A Cornish song celebrating his road locomotive, 'Going Up Camborne Hill', is believed to refer to Beacon Hill which starts at the level crossing at the London end of the station. Trevithick's birthday is celebrated with much speechifying, dancing, and band-playing each year. A statue of him holding a model of one of his engines stands outside the Public Library facing the railway station and up Beacon Hill.

Beyond Camborne was Gwinear Road, junction for Helston. Station and branch have vanished, the only vestige being an unnaturally wide level crossing.

Next stop is Hayle, an ancient town. The old foundry, now a delightful garden, was the birthplace of many of the Cornish engines. It was also a very busy port, but silting has reduced its usefulness. A sea lock at the Copperhouse head of the harbour impounded the high tide. At low water this was released in a rush to scour the channel. The sea lock can still be seen, but scouring is seldom done so silting goes on. Soon, no doubt, the channel will fill in as so many other under-used Cornish harbours have done.

Hayle Towans, some 3 miles of sandy beach and dunes, stretch away east from the town to Godrevy Lighthouse where seals can be seen basking most days. The line crosses the head of the harbour on a high, seemingly simple, viaduct. It provides unequalled views across the town, harbour, towans, and out to sea.

The train plunges under the new bypass to enter St Erth, junction for St Ives, an attractive station in the old style and currently well maintained. Unfortunately the St Ivel creamery next door, like the one at Lostwithiel has nothing to commend it aesthetically.

The line from St Erth, still very curvaceous, is mostly in cutting, so the view of St Michael's Mount is withheld from the passenger until the last moment. The train runs out of the cutting at the old Marazion Station, whose platforms have long gone but the station house remains. So, too, does the siding, not now connected, on which stand six

The end of the line. (*Photo:* Tom Heavyside)

Pullman cars converted to camping coaches. Proposals have been made to remove and renovate them as the ornate panelling inside is still intact, though the tyres have almost rusted away.

The Mount is now visible in all its glory. Owned by the National Trust, the castle is the home of Lord and Lady St Levan and the staterooms are open to visitors. The National Trust operate a restaurant which, in its first year of operation, received the Egon Ronay accolade. The Mount is accessible at low tide by a causeway over ½-mile long from the village of Marazion. At other states of the tide a fleet of small launches carries visitors to the harbour on the Mount. The boats do not always run in winter and if the tide covers the causeway when you are on the island, you are there for ten hours. A bus runs from Penzance to Marazion village, itself worth browsing round. The castle staterooms open on various weekdays according to season from April to October and it is advisable to check beforehand. The church is open for worship every Sunday and visitors are always welcome.

The train now runs close to the beach, soon passing the new carriage sheds and heliport, and halts beneath the overall roof of Penzance Station.

Penzance with a population of 20,000 is a town with much history. Humphry Davy, the great inventor, was born and went to school here. He is probably most famous for his miners' safety lamp, but this invention was only one of his many interests. Look him up in a good encyclopaedia and you will be amazed at what he was into. His statue looks down Market Jew Street from the Guildhall. (Oddly enough, Marazion also means 'Market of the Jews').

Smuggling abounded in the old days and the Admiral Benbow Inn in Church Street was a centre of the trade. On the roof lies a wax pirate armed with a pistol, ever on the look-out for the excise men. Shark-fin and Kangaroo-tail soup feature on the menu.

A diving museum of underwater treasures nearby contains artefacts and weaponry recovered from Sir Cloudesley Shovell's fleet wrecked off the Scillies. Market Jew Street is interesting but spoilt by the 'house' frontages of the big multiple stores. Go behind them into Bread Street or Coal Street and you will find the old fish cellars and warehouses.

The *Scillonian* leaves daily from the harbour, while a Hoppa minibus goes through Newlyn, Penzance's sister town and fishing port, to Mousehole, which is also worth a visit. Newlyn is an artists' paradise, and for many decades there has been a colony of painters here.

Penzance is a good centre to explore Penwith Peninsula and its great stone monuments, menhirs, quoits, and fougous, the uniquely beautiful Minack open-air theatre, the gigantic Devil's bowling stone and, of course, Land's End. Alas, the railway proposed west of Penzance never materialised, so one must make do with less interesting forms of transport.

LISKEARD—LOOE

by Clive Davies

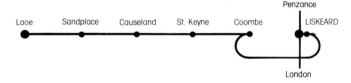

This branch, considered by some to be the prettiest in England, runs through unspoilt scenery down a deep river valley. But it has a very odd feature. After alighting from the main-line train at Liskeard, we follow the signs to the 'Looe train'; but instead of the usual bay platform we find almost a separate station with a single short platform at right angles to the main line. This branch station is north of the main line with the train heading north-east. Yet Looe is south of Liskeard, on the coast. Odd!

Trusting the train-driver, we board the train, taking care to choose a seat which has a good view through the window.

Leaving Liskeard Station, the train curves sharply to the right and passes through two short tunnels, reminiscent of the ones that boys place over their Hornby trains. The train, now heading south-west, descends, hugging the contours of the hillside. We run under a huge masonry viaduct carrying the main line east of Liskeard Station—one of many viaducts in Cornwall built to replace the original Brunel timber structures.

The train continues descending towards the bottom of the valley and after passing through some woods comes to a stop at Coombe. Immediately in front of us is a small stone bridge carrying a minor road over the railway but in the distance is another huge viaduct—the Moorswater Viaduct carrying the main line west of Liskeard Station. Our line continues and goes under the viaduct. Very odd!

We have travelled for five minutes and covered 2 miles, yet we are only ½ mile from Liskeard Station and our train is now heading north-west. However, it reverses and goes down the Looe Valley to Looe—we are getting there!

Looe (*Photo:* P. J. Sharpe)

The reason for this is that the Looe branch, like many others, was built as a goods line to carry china clay and other minerals from the Moorswater area and beyond to the harbour at Looe. The circular link to the main line was constructed later, also to carry goods from Moorswater. A direct link was ruled out because of difference in height. Even so, the link has severe gradients – up to 1 in 35 in places. Goods trains still operate from English China Clay sidings at Moorswater, but Coombe is the limit for passengers.

As Coombe is unstaffed and there is no signal-box, the operation of points and signals and the exchange of tokens has to be done by the train crew. The token (or staff) is an extra safety device, used on single-track lines; the driver must not enter a single-track section, even if the signals are clear, unless he has the token for that section. This branch has two sections: Liskeard – Coombe, which has a red-painted metal token, and Coombe – Looe, with a wood and brass token.

We now travel down the valley, its sides rising up to 300 feet from the bottom. It is thickly wooded in places with both deciduous and evergreen trees. In some places the railway goes under a canopy of greenery.

We now come to St Keyne Station, the first of the three request stops on the line. These stations are extremely small, little bigger than a bus stop. St Keyne Station is named after a village only ½ mile away but a daunting 350 feet up on top of the hill. There are few houses by the station, but close to it is the Paul Corin Musical Collection of mechanical instruments, including fairground organs and a Mighty Wurlitzer from Brighton.

We continue down the unspoilt valley. Apart from the few near the stations, there are no houses in the valley. The East Looe River, which is little more than a stream and is difficult to see because of the vegetation, grows bigger as tributaries from side valleys join it. From the train, the author has seen dragonflies along the banks of the river.

At Sandplace Station there is an attractive row of cottages to the left. The river starts to widen and ½-mile further becomes tidal. In some places there is so little room in the valley that the railway is actually built on a causeway in the river. This can best be seen from the front or rear of the older type trains. The river widens to about 200 yards and we are on its east bank. Ahead can be seen West Looe and the bridge. As we slow down to stop at Looe Station, the West Looe River can be seen on the right where it joins the East Looe River.

From the station it is 400 yards to the bridge. Originally the line continued to the bridge for goods traffic only and beyond along the quay almost to the beach as a tramway.

The small town of Looe stretches along both banks of the estuary and up the very steep hillsides. It was once a busy and prosperous port, exporting Cornish minerals and importing wine and other goods from France.

The shops and sandy beach are in East Looe. Hannafore beach is a pebble beach in West Looe, uncovered at low tide. In addition to the bridge, there is a passenger ferry across the river, using small boats. At low tide the boatmen wade across pushing the boats.

One can walk from the bridge to the beach along the Quay, observing fishing-boats and other small craft, or along Fore Street, which is lined by many small shops. Near the beach is a maze of narrow streets and whitewashed fishermen's cottages, many now converted to guest houses. Here in Higher Market Street is the Old Guildhall, built in 1500 but later rebuilt in 1872 and now a museum.

The seafront can be a *little* disappointing. The beach is rather small and the promenade has one or two ugly modern buildings. But at low tide there is sand for the children, and always the sight of the coast of Cornwall sweeping round Whitsand Bay to Rame Head in the distance, framing this pleasant place for summer holidays, a Cornish harbour town a world away from home 'up-country'.

PAR–NEWQUAY

by Graham Townsend

The line from Par to Newquay, going for 20¾ miles across the Duchy from coast to coast, is the longest of the Cornish branches. Its origins lie in the first half of the nineteenth century when J. T. Treffry of Fowey (who died in 1850) built several rail and tramways, in order to transport minerals (iron ore, china clay, and granite) from inland mines to quarries and harbours on the coast — Newquay to the north, Par and Fowey to the south. Indeed, it was only later, when this traffic declined, that thoughts turned to passengers, and the Cornwall Mineral Railway (as it then was) opened a direct passenger service from Newquay to Fowey in 1876. The section from Par to Fowey has recently been converted to a lorry-way, so it is no longer possible to reach Fowey by train from this direction, but there is a good bus service from the station at Par.

Leaving the island platform at Par, the Newquay line curves sharply to the right to join the original CMR line and pass through its now-disused station at St Blazey, next to which the locomotive depot serving this area is still situated. The train proceeds over two level crossings and then ascends the wooded Lux Valley. Here the line curves back and forth, the gradient is severe, and the train passes under the slender stone Treffry Viaduct which is 650 feet long and 98 feet high and which carried an earlier tramway across the valley. It also doubled as an aqueduct, the water running under the rails, and is a fine monument to a man who was an outstanding figure in the Cornwall of his time.

Luxulyan is the first halt, serving a small village on the edge of the high land, and the view from the train now changes quite dramatically. We shortly reach a passing loop at Goonbarrow Junction, where lines branch off to the left to the china-clay pits, which industry dominates the area – huge waste pyramids on the skyline and white dust on the signal box. Just before entering Bugle Halt, to the left, is the football field where each June is held the West of England Band Festival – a notable event in the brass-band calendar.

The line continues past Roche – another halt which, like Bugle, serves mining villages. Roche takes its name from a dramatic outcrop of granite to the south-east of the village, on top of which is St Michael's Chapel, built in 1409. The line makes a short ascent before

Newquay train passes under the Treffrey Viaduct. (*Photo:* Tom Heavyside)

crossing over, and then running alongside, the busy A30 road across the Goss Moor. A scene from the pre-war film *The Rake's Progress* was shot here, showing a youthful Rex Harrison in an open sports car waving goodbye to his wife on the train.

At the end of the moor is the other passing loop, at St Dennis Junction, but the china-clay lines which used to branch off here are no longer in operation. We now have long wide views across the breezy plateau as we round a curve and run down through two more halts, St Columb Road and Quintrell Downs.

The houses of Newquay can now be seen in the distance, and soon we are crossing over Trenance Viaduct, rebuilt for the second time in 1946, into the three-platform terminus at Newquay. For a branch terminus serving a town of 12,000 people this is quite a well-equipped station, its frontage rebuilt in the 1970s as part of a shopping development.

Newquay is one of the West Country's leading holiday resorts, noted for its excellent beaches, two of which—Tolcarne and Great Western—are within yards of the railway station. A frequent service of Hoppa minibuses giving access to all parts of Newquay from outside the station, and other buses go to Watergate Bay, Mawgan Porth, and Perranporth.

There used to be a rail extension from the station to the harbour, and the old track is now a direct pedestrian way to the bus station and shopping precinct. This line entered the harbour by a tunnel which now houses an aquarium. The Tourist Information Centre at Morfa Hall is usefully situated close to the railway station.

The Newquay branch has a basic service of six trains in each direction on weekdays, taking about fifty minutes, augmented on summer Saturdays by through trains to and from Paddington, Newcastle, Manchester, etc. At the moment there is no Sunday service except for a few weeks in the high summer. A trip on the branch not only provides an excellent means of getting to Newquay, avoiding congested roads, but also gives a fascinating glimpse of present-day Cornwall, with many interesting reminders of the Duchy's industrial history.

TRURO–FALMOUTH
by Noel Sloman

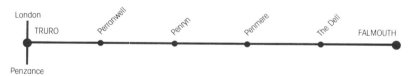

The Falmouth train leaves Truro from the bay Platform 1. It passes through the Highertown Tunnel, immediately diverges from the main line, and heads south. To the left can be seen the earthworks of the original West Cornwall Railway line which ran into the riverside station at Newham before the Great Western Railway built the present station. On the right can be seen County Hall—which some regard as a concrete monstrosity.

The embankment across the valley, on which the Skipper diesel multiple-unit is now running, was once a wooden Brunel-type viaduct. Most were rebuilt in stone, but this one was filled in. After a short tunnel, the train runs on to an embankment and then Bissoe Viaduct, which crosses the route of the Chacewater–Redruth Railway (which did not reach either place but ran from the port of Devoran to the mines round St Day and Carharrack). The course of the line can clearly be seen. The muddy tailings are the spoils of mining which are rich in tin and until the collapse of the tin price in 1985 were worth recovering. The buildings of Wheal Jane and Mount Wellington mines can be seen on opposite sides of the valley. At the time of writing, this complex is safe, but for how long is anybody's guess.

The first station on the branch is Perranwell, which once had a passing loop and a goods shed. The shed is still there. Two people have reported seeing flying saucers while waiting for trains! The Royal Oak public house is some ½-mile from the station.

After another short tunnel, the train descends to Penryn, once the site of the second loop and exceedingly busy goods yard, the latter now a car auction. A tragic event marred the closure of Penryn signal-box. After locking his box for the last time, the signalman walked along the track and jumped to his death from the viaduct.

It is this viaduct which gives fine views of the Penryn River down to the harbour mouth. A walk down the hill brings one to the centre of Penryn, which became a town as long ago as 1216. With its medieval cottages and Georgian town houses, Penryn was declared 'An Outstanding Conservation Area' in 1976. There is much of interest to see in the narrow streets and the Town Hall Museum.

The railway continues southwards in a cutting, emerging briefly at Penmere platform before plunging into another cutting before arriving at the Dell. This unmanned halt was opened in 1970 and intended to be the passenger terminus but, as it was on a down grade, the train could not be left while the driver changed ends. As the train had, therefore, to go on to the much-reduced Falmouth Station to reverse, it was decided in 1975 to reinstate Falmouth into the timetable. One of its original three platforms is, therefore, now back in use and a booking and parcels office operates from a Portakabin. With a population of 18,000, Falmouth must be the only West Country town of its size with three 'stations' within its boundaries.

The Dell remains the most convenient station for the picturesque town centre, with the Yacht Haven and the Pier from which ferry boats ply across the great natural harbour. Gyllyngvase Beach is also best reached from The Dell, while Falmouth Station is handy for Castle Beach and the sixteenth-century Pendennis Castle which guards the harbour mouth.

A short walk from Falmouth Station brings the passenger to the viewing-point above the docks, a regular attraction for visitors and residents alike. Until 1986, a Peckett saddle-tank locomotive could be seen puffing round the docks, but this has now gone to the 'great shed in the sky'. It is planned to construct a container terminal at the mouth of the Carrick Roads, on reclaimed land seaward of the docks. The Enabling Act of Parliament has been passed, and the scheme will certainly breathe new life into the branch if it comes to fruition.

ST ERTH – ST IVES
by Clive Davies

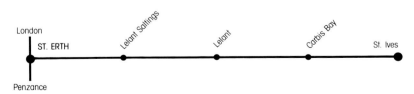

This attractive line runs alongside water—either the Hayle Estuary or the Atlantic Coast—for nearly all of its 4¾-mile length.

The line starts at St Erth, the main-line station with a bay platform for the branch train. There is a handsome stone building and the platform is decorated with hanging baskets.

When joining the train, take care to obtain a good seat with a clear view. On most lines it is debatable which side of the train has the best view, on this one there is no doubt – the best view is obtained from a forward-facing seat on the right-hand side.

Leaving St Erth we enter a cutting and emerge on the edge of the Hayle Estuary. At high tide this is a vast expanse of water, but at low tide it is covered in coarse grass with a maze of streams and hundreds of birds. The train stops. We are at Lelant Saltings – a 'park and ride' station opened in 1979. During the season, motorists can leave their car here and travel by train into St Ives, when the service is increased to approximately two trains per hour. A higher frequency would be desirable, but this would require a passing loop to be constructed in the middle of the single-track branch.

Shortly after we leave Lelant Saltings, the view is obscured by vegetation, and our next sight of the Estuary is of the silted-up Hayle harbour with the town on the far side. Then comes Lelant Station, which serves the village and is ½ mile beyond Lelant Saltings. Unfortunately trains do not usually call at both stations, so when the 'park and ride' scheme is in operation the service at Lelant is sparse.

The train enters a rock cutting and emerges 75 feet above sea-level with a superb view

Carbis Bay. (*Photo:* Tom Heavyside)

of the whole of St Ives Bay. In front, in the distance, is St Ives Head, St Ives Harbour, and part of the town. Most of the houses are hidden by Porthminster Point, a section of coast owned by the National Trust. Nearer to us is the headland of Carrack Gladden, and below us are Porth Kidney Sands. If the tide is out, this is a great expanse of white sand, which will be deserted because access is extremely difficult and the mouth of the River Hayle makes it dangerous for bathers. Over the right shoulder can be seen the mouth of the river and the beach and sand-dunes of Towans stretching for 3½ miles to Godrevvy Point, another headland owned by the National Trust. Also visible is Godrevvy Lighthouse on an island about ¼ mile offshore. This section of coast receives the full force of the Atlantic rollers and white water can often be seen round Godrevvy Point and the lighthouse, even at this distance.

We now follow the coast to St Ives. The train continues to climb and passes through Carrack Gladden in deep cutting before falling to Carbis Bay Station, close to a good sandy beach. The train follows the cliff to Porthminster Point, where it turns first to the left and then to the right over a viaduct and comes to a halt in St Ives Station.

The station is on a cliffside ledge, but most of the site has been converted into a car park. Below the station is Porthminster beach and above is the main road and a small public garden where there are seats, coin-operated telescopes, and a fine view of the harbour and bay. To reach the harbour one can go through the gap in the wall opposite the station, then left, and walk along the Warren, a narrow lane near the sea. Alternatively, one may follow the road out of the station, turn right and use the main road into the town centre.

St Ives is a small town and fishing port, with narrow hilly cobbled lanes and white-washed stone cottages, some of which have outside stone stairs. In the summer these are often decorated with hanging baskets and, because there is nowhere else to put them, lines of washing. The town is built on a small peninsula known locally as 'The Island', and up the adjoining hillsides and cliffs using every available flat space.

Two stone piers shelter a small harbour. When the tide is out, instead of the expected mud the harbour reveals a fine sandy south-facing beach. The lifeboat station, near the West Pier, is open to the public. The lifeboat is important because its area includes the treacherous coastline of the Land's End Peninsula and it has saved many lives. Further beaches are Porthmeor, facing north and suitable for surfing, and tiny Porthwidden.

Thanks to its quaintness, the surrounding countryside, and the 'quality of light', St Ives became popular with artists, in particular Whistler and Sickert, and an artists' colony was established. Barbara Hepworth lived here and some of her works can be seen in the Barbara Hepworth Museum.

Even today, one can find near the harbour and in the back lanes artists at work in their studios. One even makes pictures from bits of clocks, watches, and other household items. There are several art galleries, many small shops and, in Fore Street, the Barnes Museum of Cinematography.

FURTHER INFORMATION

Tourist Boards
Almost all of the area covered by this book is served by the **West Country Tourist Board,** Trinity Court, 37 Severnhay East, Exeter, Devon EX1 1QS (tel. 0392–76351).

The eastern part of Dorset, however, is served by the **Southern Tourist Board,** The Old Town Hall, Leigh Road, Eastleigh, Hants. SO5 4DE (tel. 0703–616027).

Timetables and leaflets
British Rail publish a passenger timetable for the whole country, of some 1400 pages, in May and September each year. It can be bought at staffed stations and at booksellers, and is usually available at public libraries.

Staffed stations and British Rail Travel Agents can also supply, free of charge, timetable booklets and leaflets for individual lines or groups of lines; leaflets about special offers, Railcards, taking bicycles by train, etc.

Maps
The Ordnance Survey publish maps of various scales, each series suited for particular purposes. For further details, write to Information and Public Inquiries, Ordnance Survey, Romsey Road, Maybush, Southampton SO9 4DH.

Also very useful are the maps in the National series (⅝ inch to 1 mile) published by John Batholomew & Sons Ltd, Duncan Street, Edinburgh EH9 1TA.

Bus services
Deregulation of bus services was introduced under the 1986 Transport Act. As a result, information about bus services given in a guidebook of this kind may soon become out of date, and we cannot accept any responsibility for changes that may have occurred since we went to press in January 1987.

However, the following bus companies were operating important services in the South West at the time, and we advise you to contact them for up-to-date information and timetables:

Bow Belle Coaches, Clew Cready, Mill Street, Crediton, Devon, EX17 1EZ (tel. Crediton 2935).
Bristol Omnibus Co. Ltd, Berkeley House, Lawrence Hill, Bristol, BS5 0DZ (tel. 558211).
Devon General Ltd, Belgrave Road, Exeter, Devon, EX1 2AJ (tel. 56231).
W. J. O. Jennings Ltd, Lansdowne Road, Bude, Cornwall, EX23 8BN (tel. 2359).
Plymouth City Transport, Milehouse, Plymouth, PL3 4AA (tel. 668000).
Red Bus Ltd, Bus Station, The Strand, Barnstaple, Devon, EX31 1EU (tel. 45444).
Southern National Ltd, 31 St James Street, Taunton, Somerset, TA1 3AF (tel. Taunton 72033; Yeovil 76233; Weymouth 783645).
Western National Ltd, Cornwall Busways, Bus Station, Lemon Quay, Truro, Cornwall, TR1 2LW (tel. Truro 2814; Penzance 69469; Plymouth 664013).
Wilts & Dorset Bus Co. Ltd, Towngate House, 2-8 Parkstone Road, Poole, Dorset, BH15 2PR (tel. Bournemouth 680888).

Train information
The principal station information offices in the South West are:

Barnstaple	0721–45991	St Austell	0726–75671
Bath	0225–63075	Taunton	0823–83444
Bristol	0272–294255	Torquay	0803–25911
Exeter	0392–33551	Truro	0872–76244
Penzance	0736–65831	Weston-super-Mare	0934–21131/2/3
Plymouth	0752–221300	Yeovil	0935–21061

WHAT IS THE RAILWAY DEVELOPMENT SOCIETY?

The **Railway Development Society** is a national, voluntary, independent body which campaigns for better rail services, for both passengers and freight, and greater use of rail transport.

It publishes books and papers, holds meetings and exhibitions, sometimes runs special trains, and generally endeavours to put the case for rail to politicians, civil servants, commerce, and industry; as well as feeding users' comments and suggestions to British Rail management and unions.

The RDS has fifteen branches covering the whole of Great Britain. The South West Branch covers Devon and Cornwall; the Wessex Branch embraces Dorset, Hampshire, the Isle of Wight, and South Wiltshire; while the rest of Wiltshire, Somerset, Avon, and Gloucestershire are the responsibility of the Severnside Branch.

Membership is open to all who are in general agreement with the aims of the society and subscriptions (summer 1987) are:
Standard rate: £7.50
Pensioners, students, unemployed: £4.00
Families: £7.50 (plus £1 for each member of household)

Write to the National Membership Secretary, Mr F. J. Hastilow, 21 Norfolk Road, Sutton Coldfield, West Midlands, B75 6SQ.

For other information about the society and its branches, write to the General Secretary, Mr T. J. Garrod, 15 Clapham Road, Lowestoft, Suffolk, NR13 1RQ.

Throughout Great Britain are also scores of local rail users' groups, most of which are affiliated to RDS. In the South West, the following groups are active:

Falmouth Line Users' Association. Founded in 1984. Secretary: Arthur Hatter, 20 Greenwood Road, Penryn, Falmouth, Cornwall, TR10 8RF.

Frome Public Transport Users' Association. Formed in 1977 and campaigned for a through train to Paddington (introduced in 1986) and to reverse the decline in local public transport. Subscriptions £2 per annum. Secretary: Gerald Quartley, 26 Butts Hill, Frome, Somerset, BA11 1HX.

North Devon Railway Line Development Group. Formed in 1978 to promote and improve the Exeter–Barnstaple service. Secretary: Ian Dinmore, 33 Charles Street, Barnstaple, Devon, EX32 7BG.

Severn Beach Line Passenger Association. Campaigns to improve service and sometimes runs special trains. Subscriptions £2 per annum (families £2.50). Details: 2 Nibley Road, Shirehampton, Bristol, BS11 9XR.

Tamar Valley Rail Development Group. The group campaigns for promotion and improvement of Plymouth–Gunnislake line. Secretary: Clive A. Charlton, Moorlands, Station Hill, Bere Ferrers, Yelverton, Devon, PL2 7JS.

OTHER BOOKS IN THIS SERIES

East Anglia by Rail
Midlands by Rail
North East by Rail
Five Shires by Rail
Cheshire and North Wales by Rail
Kent and East Sussex by Rail
Yorkshire by Rail
Lancashire and Cumbria by Rail
Scotland by Rail

All the above are obtainable from the RDS Sales Officer, Geoff Kent, 21 Fleetwind Drive, East Hunsbury, Northampton, NN4 0ST, from the respective local branches, from bookshops, or from the publishers, Jarrold Colour Publications, Barrack Street, Norwich NR3 1TR.

INDEX

Avoncliffe 21
Avonmouth 19, 20
Axminster 12

Barnstaple 35
Bath 20
Bedminster 5
Bere Alston 46
Bere Ferrers 45
Bishops Lydeard 26
Blue Anchor 29
Bodmin 49
Bournemouth 13, 14
Bradford-on-Avon 21
Bridgwater 6, 7
Bristol 5, 16-20
Bruton 9
Buckfastleigh 42
Bugle 57

Calstock 46-7
Camborne 52
Carbis Bay 60
Castle Cary 9, 24
Chapelton 35
Chesil Beach 16
Chetnole 25
Churston 39
Clifton 18, 19
Coombe 55
Crediton 33
Crewkerne 12
Crowcombe 26

Dartmouth 40
Dawlish 36
Devonport 44, 45
Dilton Marsh 22
Dorchester 15, 16
Dunster 29

Eggesford 34-5
Exeter 8, 13, 30, 35
Exmouth 32, 33, 36
Exton 32

Falmouth 59
Feniton 13
Frome 9

Gillingham 11
Gunnislake 48

Hamworthy 14
Hayle 52, 60
Highbridge 6
Honiton 13

Keyham 45
Keynsham 20
Kingswear 40

Lapford 34
Lelant 60
Liskeard 49, 54
Looe 56
Lostwithiel 49
Luxulyan 57
Lyme Regis 12
Lympstone 32

Maiden Newton 25
Marazion 53, 54
Melksham 21
Minehead 26, 29
Morchard Road 34
Moreton 15

Nailsea 5
Newquay 58
Newton Abbot 37
Newton St. Cyres 33

Paignton 37-9
Par 49, 56
Parson Street 5
Penmere 59
Penryn 59
Penzance 53-4
Perranwell 59
Pinhoe 13
Plymouth 38, 42-5
Polsloe Bridge 31
Poole 14
Portland 16
Portsmouth Arms 35

Quintrel Downs 58

Redland 19
Redruth 52
Roche 57

St. Austell 51
St. Budeaux 45
St. Columb Road 58
St. Erth 52, 60

St. Ives 60
St. Keyne 55
St. Michael's Mount 53
Salisbury 11, 21
Saltash 42-3
Sandplace 56
Sea Mills 19
Seaton 12
Severn Beach 19
Sherborne 11
Shirehampton 19
Somerton 9
Starcross 36
Staverton 41-2
Stogumber 28
Swanage 22, 23

Taunton 7, 26
Teignmouth 37
Templecombe 11
Thornford 25
Tisbury 11
Tiverton 8
Topsham 31
Torquay 37
Totnes 37, 41
Trowbridge 21
Truro 51, 58

Umberleigh 35
Upwey 16

Wareham 14
Warminster 22
Washford 28
Watchet 28
Wellington 7
Westbury 9, 21-2
Weston-super-Mare 5-6
Weymouth 16
Whimple 13
Williton 28
Wilton 11, 21
Wool 13

Yatton 5
Yeoford 34
Yeovil 11-12
Yetminster 25

ISBN 0-7117-0298-5
© 1987 Railway Development Society
Published and printed in Great Britain by Jarrold and Sons Ltd, Norwich. 187.